The Narrow Path

A Roadmap to Mature Discipleship

TOMMY HAMOR

LAYMAN2LAYMAN
DISCIPLESHIP SERIES - BOOK 1

Clay Bridges
PRESS

THE NARROW PATH: A Roadmap to Mature Discipleship

Published by Clay Bridges Press in Houston, TX
www.ClayBridgesPress.com

Design and Production by Tommy Hamor
Author's photo by Katy Cartland Photography

All emphasis in scripture quotations has been added by the author.

ISBN: 978-1-68488-177-2 (paperback)
ISBN: 978-1-68488-178-9 (hardback)
eISBN: 978-1-68488-179-6

Special Sales: Most Clay Bridges titles are available in special quantity discounts. Custom imprinting or excerpting can also be done to fit special needs. Contact Clay Bridges at Info@ClayBridgesPress.com

Dedicated to:

Pastor Mark Harris
Tucson, Arizona

In 1989 Mark saw something in me I did not yet see in myself. As a result he challenged me and mentored me in cultivating my gift and my teaching ministry at its start. Thank you!

Table of Contents

Chapter One

"Your fingerprints and DNA are not the same as anyone else's. Indeed, in the whole world it is unique, as a result of God's explicit design for you as an individual."

–Alistair Begg

More Than....

I wonder if you, like me, enjoy a good sleight-of-hand trick. A well performed demonstration never fails to amaze, specifically at the manual dexterity that goes into a successful card trick or disappearing coin trick. I hope you appreciate those things as well as I do because I have done a little sleight-of-hand here myself, something a little unusual: I've transformed what would normally be considered the "Preface" or "Forward" into *more than* a preface... actually "Chapter One".

A good practitioner of legerdemain has several methods that enable him to successfully perform one of these tricks. Distraction is a key, getting you to pay attention to what seems to be the least important thing going on. Next, there is what some call the "pass". Imagine that you have been asked to select a card, memorize the card and then place it back where you want in the deck. The "pass" is that integral part where the illusionist moves the card from where you put it to where he wants it so he can finalize the trick.

I have employed a similar "pass" because, like me, you might be one of those people who generally skips past the preface or forward and proceeds directly to page one of Chapter One. I have attempted to redirect your normal tendencies because I believe there is something fundamentally important for you to understand in order to get the maximum benefit from the topics on the following pages. So, trickery aside, let's plunge in.

At the outset, let me just say to you reading this book that if you are seminary-trained and/or a vocational minister, this book is not really intended for you. Don't get me wrong! I am thankful and very pleased you are reading it and I hope you find things in here beneficial to you and the people you shepherd. Further, I hope it will be a meaningful enough work that you would recommend it to those you feel need to hear the ideas and truths expressed herein.

However, my target audience for this book is the same as yours: the laymen and laywomen who make up the majority of the Church and para-church ministries. It is defined as those who have been born again in Christ and are embarking on the road to sanctification and maturity, those who are beginning to wonder: *"How do I become useful to God and the kingdom work He has prepared in advance for me to take part in, and in which I am to bear much fruit?"* Or, those who have been walking this path for a while but are snagged on a seemingly impassable part and are bogged down or stagnating in a journey that should be filled with movement and momentum.

The difference between this book, and perhaps others you have read, is that my message is from the perspective of another layman as opposed to the message coming from a scholar or seminary-trained minister. My motivation may be best expressed by quoting D. T. Niles, a Sri Lankan pastor in the mid 1900's, "I am just one beggar telling another beggar how to find food."

I am confident that if you search the aisles of your favorite Christian bookstore, or even the Christian category on Amazon's website or some other online bookseller, you will find numerous great books on the subject of discipleship written by pastors, ministers and scholars, each one replete with expressions of Holy Spirit-inspired teaching. These are often punctuated by learning attained through formal training and ministry experience. I have read many of those books and found them to be a great aid to my walk and my understanding of my involvement in God's plan.

I am hoping you will find this book to be equally beneficial. But I feel compelled to advise you that what you will read between these covers is distinctly and intentionally from the perspective and experience of a layman. While the initial temptation might normally be to wonder if this is a product solely of self-training, the truth is I have benefited greatly from the teaching and training of others. But in writing this book, I believe there is value in adding to those distinguished scholarly authors the voice of someone who has walked this path that every layman walks. After all, just a review of the writers of the 66 books of the bible proves that the Holy Spirit provides guidance through many types of individuals. In this case, I hope I can add something meaningful by virtue of my experience of sifting through both the teaching of the bible as well as the voices of many scholarly authors. The result for me has been to experience a body of belief that totally reflects God's truth and fits me organically.

In this way, when I embark on kingdom work, I do so naturally as the layman Tommy Hamor instead of trying to parrot my favorite preacher, scholar or author. For me that is one of the essential keys to becoming who God intended me to be and what I know you would like to be able to say about your own life in Christ.

Anticipation

The topic of discipleship yields itself to understanding what is expected, what is required, and what is waiting for the believer as he or she grows into that entrusted disciple that delights the heart of God. For that, some need a primer...a simplified, understandable explanation of this process that occurs during our sanctification that can become a roadmap for how to navigate through the teachings, the experiences, the challenges and the events that embody our discipleship experience.

I felt it was important to write in this manner of layman to layman after sitting in many small groups, bible studies and informal conversations where good, devoted believers have struggled with the issues involved in maturing as a disciple without the opportunity of years of formal theological training or vocational ministry experience. Understand that my intention in continuing to refer to this type of formal training is certainly not meant to minimize the need for those things anymore than it is meant to characterize those things as absolute requirements for Christian growth. The bible commands us to give double honor to those who serve among us, for both their service and their efforts in preparing for that service. But clearly, as we gaze into the words of the New Testament, there is ample evidence that God desires to fully develop *all* men and women (hereafter collectively referred to as "laymen" to distinguish them from those who are vocationally involved in ministry) and engage them in His work as mature disciples.

In the American church, statistics tell us that for every vocational minister there are more than 100 laymen whose contributions to the advancement of the kingdom are just as necessary and just as expected by our Lord as those who we often consider to be "professionals". So how do we, as laymen, contribute to this process? In 1 Corinthians 3:9, God declares that we are His fellow workers and He has invited us to be a part of what He is doing in the world. Certainly a good part of that is to mature us and conform us to the image of His Son, in addition to equipping us for His service.

What I have discovered is that there are many wonderful resources that can inform us as to the "*what*" that is important to this journey, but there often tends to be only a vague impression conveyed in the Church as to the "*how*". My intent in providing this discipleship roadmap for laymen, is that you, the reader, will be encouraged to take that next step, no matter where on the continuum of discipleship development you currently stand.

In the interest, then, of not "burying the lead", my prayer for this book is to spur you on to spending more time investigating God's Word and pursuing the topic of discipleship in order to make it manifest in your life. As you do that, I hope you develop the habit of asking yourself good, honest questions about what you believe and why you believe it as you mature in your faith. The result of this effort will no doubt be the discovery of ways you can be an active, indispensable part of the kingdom that is "here and not yet". There is still much work to be done in advancing God's kingdom and each of us plays an integral part in the accomplishment of His sovereign plan.

Questions for Consideration

At the end of each of the subsequent chapters, you will find three questions with the following corresponding icons:

The first icon is a tuning fork. Just as the tuning fork is designed to produce a one note resonance, this icon and corresponding question are meant to guide you toward thinking about the most important idea or thought that continues to resonate from the chapter.

The second icon is a candle whose corresponding question suggests a focus on something new learned in the chapter, perhaps an "*aha*" moment. This could be an idea brand new to your way of thinking, a magnified understanding of an idea you were already somewhat familiar with, or just a fresh perspective on a truth revisited.

Finally, the last icon is a stethoscope, which demands a look inward, providing introspection and reflection into some thought in the chapter that has the chance to begin changing you from the inside out.

Use these questions in a small group if you like or just as a private way of reviewing what you have previously learned from this reading. The habit of utilizing these questions will enhance your learning and prepare you for the next chapter.

Chapter Two

"The Church is the place that our dreams are crushed. And that is a good thing"

–Dietrich Bonhoeffer

Initiation

Somewhere rambling around in the memory banks of my mind is an image of a vintage David Carradine Kung-Fu western scene from the early 1970's television series. It pictures the old Shaolin monk mentoring the young pupil Caine as he seeks to make sense of all the cryptic teachings of this martial arts discipline.

"Grasshopper, when you can snatch the pebble from my hand, only then will you be able to walk the narrow path".

The Narrow Path.

Or just as likely, in a less dated reference, I can imagine it as a phrase attributed to anything from the goal of new age enlightenment to the latest weight loss craze. Countless teachers, mentors and motivational speakers have undoubtedly co-opted this phrase and slapped it on whatever they were hawking, with the goal of making us better people. But I suspect that you and I really are not interested in "***a***" narrow path. Instead, we are desperate for "***the***" narrow path.

It is that one path for which we were destined, indeed for which we were created, that will ultimately result in peace, contentment, and fulfillment and the surety that in these three score years and ten that we live we will not have missed the purpose of this life. It is no doubt a universal condition that each of us, as we prepare to close our eyes that final time, will yearn to make sure we have lived out that purpose, that there has been a good reason for all we have enjoyed and endured.

The narrow path we are searching for is none other than the one Jesus spoke specifically about only once, and which the remainder of the New Testament devoted its energies toward exhorting us to adopt. This narrow path is held out as something mysterious and potentially difficult and yet it is calling to us across the millennia since Christ uttered the words in the greatest sermon He ever preached, which we know as the Sermon on the Mount.

> 13 *"Enter through the narrow gate. For wide is the gate and broad is the road that leads to destruction, and many enter through it.* 14 *But small is the gate and narrow the road that leads to life, and only a few find it."* Matthew 7: 13-14

The King James Version of the bible calls the path "*the narrow way*". The English Standard Version simply "*the way that is hard*".

Other translations, like the NIV example here, abbreviate it as "the road" that is narrow, or others just "the way". Whatever translation you favor, two ideas are clear:

- There is a designed, preordained path.

- There is a difficulty to it that we must be warned about, and there is uncertainty that requires clarifying, even as Jesus is instructing us in how to find that path.

Of course, finding secure footing on the narrow path is typically a secondary message in the teaching of this great passage. No matter how many sermons I have heard on this passage or commentaries I have read, the emphasis usually weighs on the gates leading to Christ's Kingdom as opposed to the characteristics of each corresponding path once entered upon.

That emphasis is not a point of criticism but rather a necessary reality. This is one of the hallmark evangelical gospel passages that boils down the circumstances that face all of mankind ever born or ever to be born: where do we find the life that is truly life as opposed to just biological existence?

Jesus says there is one obvious, easily accessed, entryway that looks deceptively like it would be good, but ends very badly, for all of eternity. Then there is a smaller, more difficult-to-find access to everlasting life, the kind of life we dare dream about, but which actually turns out to be far beyond what we could ask for or imagine.

Though harder to find, it is not actually hidden. The allure of that gate happens to stand in contradiction to the corrupted mindset of our fallen nature. As broken people (broken as in not working as intended) we want to follow the crowd. We draw our comfort from noting that a lot of other people have seen and are pursuing the same thing as we are. We breathe easier when we are running with the pack. Consequently, we equate "easier" with "better" and the broad door is certainly easier to find and simpler to access. Our adversary specializes and delights in making it so.

No, we are not hardwired to run headlong toward a smaller, harder-to-find gate that warns of difficulty on the other side. For us to actually appreciate the narrow way as the infinitely preferred path, we have to become something new... a new creation. But more on that later.

At this point you may be asking yourself why Jesus only mentioned this narrow way once and why it seems such an unexplored disclosure. Perhaps the clarifying answer is that Jesus only phrased it this way once, but spent the better part of His ministry teaching about what this meant.

And not just Jesus, but Peter and Paul and James and John and Jude and whoever wrote Hebrews (Apollos, perhaps, as Martin Luther suggests?). They all spent a good portion of their time translating their doctrinal teachings into practical life truths that monumentally impact how to navigate this narrow path once you have entered through the small gate.

The Church has a history of applying labels to important issues and beliefs. Often those labels cause more confusion than clarity. However, in this case, it is appropriate and quite important. Let me reveal the more recognizable way of describing this narrow path journey: **Discipleship**. We discover this on the narrow path that continues beyond the narrow gate. For just as the path leading to life is narrow, so also is the path that proceeds from the gate and takes us on this journey to mature discipleship. That is what this book is about.

Jesus was so committed to promoting the spiritually successful walk on the narrow path that He drew around Himself twelve people who we know as The Twelve Disciples (though there were actually many more disciples during His ministry before the Cross, these twelve were the focal point of Jesus' three year earthly ministry).

He invested nearly all of His time with them, lived life with them, gave them special insights into His teachings to the masses, and generally put them through a three year training camp. And, judging by the remainder of these disciples' lives, He had a success ratio of 92%. The blame for that one failure must be placed on Judas, not Christ. But this book is not about why one man refused to take hold of the life Jesus was offering him, but rather how the churches we attend can begin to increase their success ratio, for making and growing disciples, anywhere approaching that of Jesus'.

The stakes are high in that endeavor, for the consistent advance of the kingdom in a continuing dying world depends on increase happening. Look at the American Church – look at your local church. How many of the members live lives that reflect their willingness to go to their death to see the gospel advanced, versus how many people are content to put in their hour and a half most Sundays and feel they have played their part?

Jesus made a special point of telling the world how they would notice who was and who wasn't someone who had successfully graduated from this training camp, and then He gave them a "small" task:

Go and turn the world upside down!

Speak the very words of God!

Face death willingly at every turn for the privilege of seeing just one more soul rescued from the broad road that leads to destruction!

~

The call to discipleship was on Jesus' mind every moment of every day, and this is unusual from our perspective. We don't normally cast every event in our day in light of eternity like Jesus did. Consider the following hypothetical for a moment.

> *A man is rapidly wheeled into an emergency room. He has flatlined and there are only moments remaining to possibly restore any semblance of life. The crash cart is called for and the Emergency Room doctor and his team have jumped into a flurry of action to try and yank back this life from the abyss. The doctor makes one last check for his patient's vitals, grabs the defibrillator paddles, demands all other personnel stand clear, and then...*

Of course, this isn't much of a hypothetical. We have all observed this scene played out on television, undoubtedly some have witnessed it first hand. What we *don't* ever see is the Emergency Room doctor pausing and launching into a teaching about what he is going to do, who he is and how the world will be impacted when he accomplishes said task.

But that is exactly what Jesus did. That is the prerogative and the practice only of the Divine, when the duration of death is not a factor in the ability to re-animate a lifeless body. To illustrate this, consider the narrative in the gospel of John, chapter 11. Jesus and His disciples were away from their home base when word came that one of His dearest friends in the world was sick and near death. Unexpectedly, Jesus did not rush to his friend's bedside or even heal him from afar. In fact, he did the counter-intuitive thing.

He delayed.

In fact He delayed so long that His friend Lazarus died and had been buried for four days. Only then did Jesus go to Bethany.

Even before you read the text you can imagine the scene. At some point in our lives we have all lost someone and experienced this traumatic time ourselves. But John goes into great detail about what was happening in Bethany and what the family members were thinking. Jesus finally arrives and begins to translate doctrine into life-giving words.

He actually begins this while embarking on the road to Bethany. His disciples dutifully remind Him that there is danger upon His return to Judea, but Jesus responded with teaching about walking by the Light and then declaring that He was going to "*wake Lazarus from his deadly slumber*".

When He arrived, He is confronted by a grieving Martha, who like all of us, tended to look for someone to blame for what she perceived to be a senseless death. In this case, she intimated that it is partially Jesus' fault for not being there and providing another miraculous healing. They had witnessed such an event so often that they began to expect that healing was Jesus' "go-to" move.

Jesus responded, not by debating her on causality or responsibility, but rather with doctrine. Of course it's not much of a debate. Jesus began by comforting her, saying *"your brother will rise again"* and Martha agreed (though she was thinking doctrinally about his rising at the resurrection at the end of days). This exchange, in and of itself, is not so unusual. Any of us who have attempted to comfort someone at a funeral uses similar language. *"He's in a better place...". "She is no longer suffering...". You'll be reunited one day...".*

Jesus' intent, though, is not to leave Martha with only words of comfort. Instead, Jesus does what none of us would do in a similar setting. He speaks words intended to advance Martha's understanding of what God is really doing in this moment.

Perhaps it would be instructive to paraphrase what Jesus says next this way: "*Martha, it's time to upgrade your faith*". She has a doctrinal grasp of what resurrection is but Jesus says it is time to update that understanding, to have it illuminated by the very Light He told His disciples they must walk by. In this way resurrection is not just an idea for countless years in the future, but has a present-day reality.

> [25]*"I am the resurrection and the life. The one who believes in Me will live, even though they die;* [26] *and whoever lives by believing in me will never die".* John 11:25-26

Don't miss how Jesus punctuates that revelatory statement next with four staggering words. Even before He performs one of the most amazing miracles of His ministry. Even before He offers proof-positive that He is the absolute final authority on death and life. Even before He demonstrates the most dramatic love for a friend, He asks Martha this simple question:

"Do you believe this?"

It's tempting to run pell-mell over this simple question in your desire to see the climax of the story. But that is unwise, because, for the disciple, ***this*** is the question that will be asked of you at every illumination of truth you are introduced to along the narrow path. These are the four words we must expect to hear from the Holy Spirit all along this discipleship odyssey.

It is also the question every person considering the narrow gate over the broad gate will contend with. It is the natural, obvious question of the gospel: "*Do you believe this?*" It is the question that serves as the touchstone determining a person's eternal destination after this life, and it is the constant question of the disciple as he navigates the narrow path.

"Do you believe this?"

Jesus shows in John 11 that He is not unsympathetic with the difficulty of believing faith in the face of things we have not seen or encountered before. And so, Jesus goes all in. He steps up to the grave of Lazarus, quiets the mourners, and demands, to the glory of God, that the stone be rolled away and that death relinquish its hold on His friend Lazarus.

As silence descends over the scene, dramatic things begin to happen immediately: first, humanity raises its doubting head.

Martha, newly illuminated about the theology of the resurrection, is still an unfinished work. She is still bound up in Jewish tradition that taught that the spirit of the deceased hovers over the body for three days before making its way to the place of the dead, Sheol. Hence, Jesus' delay in returning to Bethany...to make sure no one would be able to use human reasoning to explain a divine occurrence.

Then, the unthinkable...the unbelievable. Jesus speaks these unforgettable words:

> *"Lazarus, come out!"*

And he did!

There are a couple of final things we don't want to overlook here that together double down on the expected result of this event in the lives of the witnesses in Bethany. The impact of these two things rings down through the ages just as truly to all those who have read this story that John has faithfully shared in such exquisite detail.

We should expect that someone who is seeking and searching

and investigating the claims of the bible would see something extraordinary in this man Jesus, so much so that they would hopefully realize all His claims are true and receive Him as Savior. That alone is a truth great enough to move mountains of disbelief. For those readers that may be skeptical, though, consider these two exclamation marks on this fantastic story:

First, a dead man came back to life merely because of three words spoken by Jesus; and second, all the rest of the dead in the area of that cemetery stayed in their tombs because of a single word.

Lazarus, a man four days dead, demonstrated disciple-like obedience to Jesus' command to get off his cold death bed and come back to life. And every other dead person buried in the vicinity of Jesus' voice stayed dead because He only called *"Lazarus"*.

What if He had only said *"Come out!"*? Undoubtedly, every dead person in that cemetery would have shed their grave clothes that day, too!

"Now, do you believe this?"

Questions for Discussion

When you think about the broad path versus the narrow path, what is the primary characteristic of the narrow path that fills you with hope?

How does Jesus' upgraded teaching on the resurrection make you think differently about this topic?

What areas of your belief or your traditions do you sense are going to be challenged and elicit the question "Do you believe this?"

Chapter Three

Photograph

In 2010, I joined a group of people from my church and embarked on a mission trip to the southern part of Costa Rica in order to work with a missionary family we had sent out a couple of years earlier. It would be my third mission trip to that beautiful country, but this one was slated to be quite different.

On this occasion, we were intent on making inroads into an unreached people group of indigenous Indians called the Guaymi. The Guaymi exist primarily in Panama, but also have populations in Costa Rica and most of them had never encountered non-Costa Ricans. Even more critical, they have had virtually no contact with any Christian group. The Guaymi in Costa Rica are disdained by most of the Hispanic population, and as such have been segregated to reservations in the mountainous rainforests of that country where they eke out a very meager living.

The Guaymi we were targeting for this particular trip lived in a small village approximately 3,000 feet up one of the mountains in an area not too very far from the Costa Rican/Panamanian border. The entire reservation consisted of about 3,500 Guaymi split into several villages on different levels of the mountain. The village we were involved with was Betania Arriba on the Coto Brus reservation and the only way up to the village was a rugged horse path at about a 20 to 30 degree upward slope for most of a three and a half hour hike. To make this physical challenge even more difficult, we were deluged by a torrential rainforest thunderstorm for about two and a half hours of the trek from the moment we began our climb.

My intent for the above story is to set the stage for the photograph on the previous page. I took this photo on the side of that mountain about thirty minutes after the storm ended, where the slope of the path would soon begin to flatten out a bit. After more than two and a half hours being drenched to the bone, the sun came out and the steam bath began. But all that faded into the background once I reviewed this photo that I had taken.

Immediately, in my spirit I sensed God aligning my experience teaching about discipleship for more than a decade with this very scene, providing a picture that would clearly define the characteristics of the narrow path.

Spend a minute reviewing the picture on the previous page. You'll note the very narrow, crooked path with rain puddles and mud that made the footing tenuous. What may not be clear from the angle of the photo, is that this muddy path was inundated with deep indentations made by horse hooves (and now full of rain water) and caution had to be taken just to keep a steady stride without turning an ankle.

In the background, you can see the steam or fog is preventing a very clear vision of what is ahead on the path, which is further obscured by the incline of the path that blocks out more than just a few yards of visibility of what lies over the next rise. Finally, the acute angle of the ground on either side of the narrow path threatens problems for those who are not paying very close attention to each step and wander off the path.

Hopefully, this description has allowed you to begin to get a glimpse of what I believe God was revealing through this scene in that moment about *our* narrow path. Our narrow path will require careful attention to all types of challenges that can make our discipleship journey fraught with difficulties and struggles. Further, we must shed the comfort level that comes with seeing far ahead, because on this path we will have limited vision down the road. Thankfully, God has no such limitation and is watching that unseen portion of the path for us, in His sovereignty over everything ahead of us.

Challenges on the Path

The bible informs us that the challenges we will face come to us via our three great adversaries in our life: the world (1 John 2:15), the flesh (Galatians 5:17) and the devil (John 1:30 and other passages like 2 Corinthians 4:3-4). The world represents the corrupt and fallen culture that is so very far from the Garden. When we attempt to live in a manner that is counter-cultural and is instead in alignment with God's will, we find the workings of this world opposing us firmly at every turn.

The flesh indicates our own habits and inclinations which have been the hallmarks of the way we have been living apart from what the apostle Paul calls, in his last three epistles, "sound doctrine". In addition, the flesh points to areas of our lives we have not fully surrendered to our King. Transformation, which is the precious fruit of maturing as a disciple, is what God has designed to battle this remnant of our flesh and make our journey on this path successful.

Finally, the devil. He is our greatest adversary, who engages us on a spiritual level, tempting, trying and testing us for the purpose of impeding our journey to discipleship and, in the process, fracturing our testimony and our faith. With these three working against us, it is no wonder that Jesus cautioned us about the difficulties of this most worthwhile of paths.

However, He is the great Overcomer of death who has provided for our entry through the narrow gate to real life. And it is He who is with us every step of our journey along the narrow path that precedes from the narrow gate. He is intent on making us overcomers as well and all He awaits is for us to launch our stride along this journey to maturity.

Unfortunately, many Christians do not understand this or are unsure of how to proceed. Many believers are simply loitering just inside the narrow gate, feeling this is all that is required to ensure eternal life, and then they are onto their own plan for the rest of their days on earth. Please note: there are only two plans for your life: God's plan and your plan. One is destined to fail, and - spoiler alert - it's not God's. So, if you are ready, let's dive into a look at what God has in mind for His disciples as we follow His plan and His path.

Questions for Discussion

Take a moment again to review the photo on the title page of this chapter or the front cover of the book. What resonates with you about the visual imagery of that picture? Which aspect of the path shown in the photograph strikes you as unexpected, unconsidered or especially daunting?

What new truth about the narrow path are you beginning to consider by virtue of this analogous photograph? Is this something that is challenging to what you initially believed or is it something new to consider?

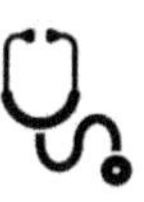

What is your next step in preparing yourself in light of something you are considering new for the first time? How does this begin to be immediately applied to your walk along the path?

CHAPTER FOUR

"The only safe place for sheep is by the side of the shepherd, because the devil does not fear the sheep; he just fears the Shepherd"

–A. W. Tozer

Sheep and Disciples

Before moving into the primary teaching of this book, I want to spend some time in this chapter drawing distinctions between our identity as a sheep in Christ's flock (which is where we all start) and the mature disciple which is our lifelong goal. In addition to that distinction, we will discover something that is of fundamental importance to the disciple.

As sheep in Jesus' flock, our emphasis is on being saved and sustained. And what a glorious place that is for us to be as we come into His fold! But as we begin to turn our attention to that idea of making a growing discipleship relationship with Christ our top priority, the emphasis changes from being cared for to being trained. We see that dramatically in the three year training Jesus gave the Twelve and we'll touch on it more when we begin to look at what it means to learn as a follower. But for the purpose of this chapter, let's explore the idea of Jesus' expectations for those in His flock.

Picturing Sheep

Josh McDowell once famously described sheep as, "dirty, dumb and defenseless". This does not make for a very endearing metaphor for those of us who are sheep in Christ's flock, but does it not describe our lives if we just think about it? What it really says about sheep is that by necessity they must be very reliant upon their shepherd; they can't feed themselves, their wool gets dirty very easily and they have no natural means of defense... they're just standing there ready to be a meal for some predator.

However, any distinction between sheep and disciples is **not** meant to be unflattering to the sheep. Becoming a part of Jesus' flock is the beginning point of our eternal journey with Him, and God is well aware of the sheep's struggles, circumstances, value and potential. It is why God provided for us a Good Shepherd.

There are more than 150 references to sheep in the Old Testament and nearly 50 more in the New. One of the most dramatic, relative to God's view of His sheep is in Ezekiel 34. In that passage God has a word for the shepherds who are not caring properly for the flocks as well as some pointed words for the sheep themselves. But again, God understands us and He ends Ezekiel 34 with a promise of blessings for the members of His flock.

Indeed, being one of the sheep in the flock under the care of the Good Shepherd is a marvelous place to be. Just one look at

David's 23rd Psalm and you'll see how he articulates his appreciation for everything that endues to him through this relationship with the Lord who is our Shepherd.

In that Psalm there is safety and provision and rest and peace and guidance through the worst situations we can imagine (even through the valley of the shadow of death). No doubt, believers are enthralled by these benefits (as they should be) but many are content to enjoy them as all there is until they die and go to heaven.

It can not be stated more strenuously that as great as being a sheep in God's flock is, that is not the finishing point of our journey, nor is that all that God intends for any of us who are followers of Christ! He has reserved for us a very special status of becoming disciples. Growing, maturing, serving, always-following disciples (contrasted with those described as disciples in John 6:66 who, at Jesus' hard teachings, *"turned back and no longer followed him"*.)

Status

I said something in that previous paragraph that I don't want you to zip past: "*very special status* ". Let me clarify what is meant by that.

Many bibles follow the tradition of capitalizing the names, pronouns and titles of Jesus Christ. The capitalization of pronouns is especially helpful in passages that have more than one "him" in them (Matthew 4:10 would be an example of multiple use of that pronoun). Unfortunately, some newer translations have departed somewhat from this practice with regard to pronouns because the corresponding words are not capitalized in the Greek texts (and the Hebrew alphabet is nothing but capitals with no lowercase letters). But many of them still capitalize titles and descriptions of Jesus as a way of distinguishing His practice in perfection versus similar roles undertaken by mortal men, which are always practiced in some degree of imperfection. Consider all the "capitalized" titles or descriptions we find in the text for Jesus which can be also used in their uncapitalized form for man:

- Lord (hundreds of examples, such as Galatians 1:3)
- Savior (example Philippians 3:20)
- Teacher (Matthew 8:19 which has both, one capitalized for Jesus and one uncapitalized for a Jewish teacher questioning Him)
- Master (example Luke 8:24)
- Messiah (example Luke 2:11)
- Overseer (example 1 Peter 2:25)
- Son, as in Son of Man (example John 5:27)

There may be others and there are certainly many descriptions attributed to Jesus that are not capitalized (e.g. "servant", "brother", and "friend" just to name a few). And there are some such as "True Vine" and "High Priest" which probably should be capitalized for clarity's sake. Even if the text does not capitalize to give the distinction, we can gather the reference to Christ either through context or because it is Jesus' self-description in the Gospels. For instance, in John 17:18 during Jesus' high priestly prayer on the night before He was crucified, He said this:

As you sent me into the world, I have sent them into the world.

The Greek for both instances of "sent' in this passage is *apostello* from which we get the English word "apostle'. It's as if Jesus was saying to His Father, that just as He was sent as an Apostle to this world, He was likewise sending His disciples out in the manner of apostles.

While this delineation of capitalized forms of words can yield understanding into how our roles should mimic Jesus', there is a more important point I want to make here about our status. I want to turn your attention to the fact that there is one title that is *never* attributed to Jesus, either in a capitalized format or non-capitalized:

Disciple!

That one, God has reserved for you and me. It is the very status He desires to offer to those Christ-followers who seek to grow beyond "sheep in the flock" status and instead embark on the journey that fulfills every plan God has for our lives.

Consider then that even though we can occupy many of these titles as well (you might be a teacher, a servant, a prophet or even an apostle), the one we *don't* share with Jesus is disciple. Jesus is never called "The Great Disciple", because, again, that is a title that is reserved especially for you. It is a title of privilege, opportunity and duty (it's like God designating you as "adopted"...a term used to impart dignity within our relationship with Him when He brings us into His family). Discovering this should ignite our desire to embark on the path to maturity.

Disciple as a Definition

"Disciple" is essentially a New Testament word, with two exceptions, and even these Old Testament passages begin to give insight into important aspects of discipleship. We see the first in Isaiah 8:16:

> *Bind up the testimony of warning and seal up God's instruction among my disciples.*

Here the word "disciples" is translated from the Hebrew word *limmud* which means "one taught". Then we see one more Old Testament reference in Isaiah 19:11:

> *The officials of Zoan are nothing but fools; the wise counselors of Pharaoh give senseless advice. How can you say to Pharaoh, I am one of the wise men, a disciple of the ancient kings"?*

In this latter passage, "disciple" is the Hebrew word *ben* which means "son" as in "Benjamin" (which, for instance, literally means "son of my right hand").

Our only Old Testament references, then, give insight to the **student** aspect as well as the **family** aspect. We see these ideas being carried forward into the New Testament in Matthew 12:47-50 where Jesus, while teaching, is told that His family is waiting to speak to Him. Jesus responds:

> [47]*Someone told him, "Your mother and brothers are standing outside, wanting to speak to you."* [48]*He replied to him, "Who is my mother, and who are my brothers?"* [49]*Pointing to his disciples, he said, "Here are my mother and my brothers.* [50] *For whoever does the will of my Father in heaven is my brother and sister and mother."*

Here Jesus carries over these two Old Testament ideas and merges the idea of student with the idea of family. This new aspect of our relationship to God begins to be displayed once Jesus' three year ministry begins with His disciples.

New Testament Usage

Even though "disciple" is essentially a New Testament word, it is only prevalent in the Gospels and the book of Acts. In fact, it is so prevalent that it is mentioned 294 times in those five books. The disciples are only mentioned once (The Twelve) in the epistles and there is a good reason for this.

The Old Testament, effectively the beginning of the progressive revelation of who we were to become, focuses on the collective, the chosen people, and calling us as the children of the Promise. But once we turn the pages to the New Testament, the individual comes into focus.

That focus begins to manifest itself with the sheep being described as saved and sustained. Then it continues to be drawn into greater clarity with the disciple being trained. Still the emphasis is on the individual. In Matthew 10:30 we read:

> *And even the very hairs of your head are all numbered.*

Here the distinction is not in numbered as in "counted", but rather as numbered as in "individually identified". As disciples, we are not grouped as a "flock", "herd", "gaggle" or any other similar collective term borrowed from nature or culture, because from the inception of Christ's work and ministry, He is drawing attention to the individual.

Finally, the epistles represent a return to the collective emphasis again, focusing on the mobilization of the Church (*this* is the only appropriate collective term for disciples). This is a critical understanding: the New Testament expects us to grasp that the Church is to be made up of a whole host of individuals who are maturing disciples. This is the mission statement of the church, so much so that Jesus codified it into His Great Commission when He instructed us to go into the nations and *make disciples of all people.*

Distinguishing Disciples

One of the most important first steps in studying about discipleship is landing on the primary differentiations between sheep and disciples. The teaching of Christ Himself makes those distinctions and the way we are first alerted to them is to differentiate between causation and motivation.

All who believe are sheep in the flock of our Great Shepherd, Jesus Christ. Becoming a sheep is a **result of** salvation. That is a causative statement.

Sheep are obliged and expected to grow into disciples (though many do not). Becoming a disciple is a **response to** salvation. That is a statement describing motivation.

Further, there is another important way to illuminate when the sheep have begun to take on the role of growing disciples. It is a question of contrasting their focus. Sheep focus on **their own needs** (consider, again, the view of the shepherd in the 23rd Psalm):

- Very first verse focuses on "wants"
- Quiet waters are expressed as a need of the sheep to be supplied by the shepherd because sheep are deathly afraid of moving water (the shepherd will take stones and dam up the river or stream to create a quiet pool).
- Sheep cannot find foraging spots for themselves, so it is

incumbent on the shepherd to lead them to a place to eat. In doing so, we see the shepherd will pour oil down holes that are the homes of deadly brown adders to prevent them from biting the noses of sheep as they bend their head to graze.
- Sheep suffer from another pest in the nose fly which will lay eggs in the mucus membranes of the sheep's nose. The shepherd "anoints their heads with oil" in a proactive medicinal manner to protect sheep from this irritant and keep them from being driven to great lengths to combat the aggravation from the fly hatchlings which move up from the nose into the sheep's brain.

On the other hand, disciples learn to focus on **others' needs**. Let's observe the training Jesus gave them by His own example.

- Teaching
- Preaching
- Healing
- Showing compassion
- Leading (shepherding those under your care)
- Serving with correct motivation.

And if anyone gives even a cup of cold water to one of these little ones ***who is my disciple****, I tell you the truth, that person will certainly not lose their reward." Matthew 10:42*

Reflexes

How will those seeking to grow along this path be able to

determine when they are turning the corner from simply sheep in the flock to maturing disciples? Hopefully, this will become apparent in the following pages as we begin to delve deep into the specifics of the path we are on.

However, one thing will begin to be noticeable. That is this: the things we initially did by duty or discipline begin to be the things we now do by reflex. The actions and behaviors that mark the disciple become natural, organic.

When I was a child, our church provided personalized giving envelopes to every member, even children. This was the first way that the church began to instill the duty of tithing to us in our youth. On that envelope would be check boxes that were reminders of other things as well that we should be learning to do:

Did you read your bible every day?
Did you memorize a bible verse?
Did you invite someone to church?
Did you attend the worship service?
Did you tithe of your earnings?
Did you share the Gospel with someone this week?

These "checkboxes" were not being tallied on some official record. They were merely designed as lessons to instruct and remind each person what a follower of Jesus dutifully did.

Now, as an adult disciple, do I need this kind of subtle reminder? I shouldn't. These good behaviors that were being instilled in me as a child are now things that come organically to me. I do these things by reflex, motivated by my gratitude for all Jesus has done for me. They are the most natural things in the world for me to do as a disciple of my Savior.

Where are you today? Is your current instinct or reflex toward naturally doing the things Jesus did Himself and what He instilled in His followers, or do you find that you are still having to discipline yourself to do the things Jesus requires of His disciples? Are you imitating Christ by reflex or by effort? The checkbox mentality can only carry you so far and is inadequate in taking you to the level to which you desire to ascend. In the chapters that follow we will take a look at how we can approach this journey in a way that is beneficial to this goal.

Cautionary Words for the Disciple

Before we leave this chapter, though, let's consider some cautionary words regarding growing as a disciple. As much as we would like to read only positive references in the bible to this special status we want to live out as mature disciples, unfortunately, not every reference to a disciple or disciples is very complimentary. Setting our initial focus primarily on the Gospels, we find these illuminating cautionary tales.

In Matthew 15 we encounter the Syrophoenician woman (also called a Canaanite woman), who came crying out to Jesus for her demon-possessed daughter. Initially, Jesus did not answer her a word. So his disciples came to him and urged him into action.

> *"Send her away, for she keeps crying out after us."* Matthew 15:23

Sadly, disciples often display this type of uncaring attitude in the face of real need, especially with people who are not like them. This can be indicative of our growth in discipleship continuing to be impinged upon by the world, the flesh or the devil. Jesus completed His teaching here by healing the daughter because of the mother's faith, despite the fact that she was not a Jew and in doing so also alerted His disciples to a continuing challenge with regard to their growth.

One chapter later in Matthew 16, when Jesus was alone with his disciples and speaking to them about His coming death, Peter launched into a rebuke to which Jesus, turning to Peter said:

> *"Get behind me, Satan! You are a stumbling block to me; you do not have in mind the things of God, but the things of men."* Matthew 16:23

Disciples can sometimes tend to focus too often on the things of the world and thereby impede kingdom movement and message. This represents a classic "what I want" versus "what God wants" tension that is yet another challenge that makes the narrow path difficult.

Finally, one last example, also in Matthew (chapter 14). This touchstone passage is in verses 22-36 where we observe the disciples leaving the feeding of the 5,000 miracle and setting out by boat, at Jesus' command, on the Sea of Galilee. There, they are caught up in a massive storm for the entire night. This passage puts on display one of the most awe-inspiring pictures of Jesus as He walks out on the stormy sea toward the struggling disciples who initially confused Jesus for a ghost.

Someone once said, *"In eight hours the disciples went from spiritual to spiritists"*. That seems a very apt encapsulation of what happened. The disciples went from a high of the miraculous feeding of the 5,000 from five loaves and two fishes to the low of decrying Jesus as a specter, out of their irrational fear. Disciples often vacillate between the highs and lows instead of being consistent. This is perhaps one of the hardest things for a Christian disciple to overcome in this world. Only growth as God the Father intends rescues us from a life of inconsistency. The following chapters demonstrate the manner in which God lovingly guides us along this path to growth.

Questions for Discussion

What attribute that differentiates the disciple from the sheep resonated with you?

What new truth was illuminated in this last chapter? In particular, do you look at the distinction between sheep and disciples any differently now?

As you reflect on the differences between sheep and disciples, would you describe yourself as a selfish believer or a selfless believer? Are you a consumer of the things available in the Church or are you a dispenser?

Chapter Five

"Mountaintops are for views and inspiration,
but fruit is grown in the valleys."
–Billy Graham

FLAIR

A few years ago, I took an online IQ test. There are many of these available and some are not worth the time you would devote to carefully considering and answering the questions. This one, however, originated from a reputable organization that was generally concerned about accuracy and methods. So I invested the time, answered a huge number of questions and came back with an IQ of 140. That was pleasant to see, but admittedly I was hesitant to immediately sign up for Mensa.

I can remember reading in a psychology book in college that the best time to assess one's IQ was at the age of six, presumably because your brain is not yet cluttered with millions of trivial facts, misconceptions and untrue assertions. I am well past that age and my brain is indeed crammed with borderline useless trivia, uncertain thinking and even sound things that are unnecessary to my spiritual growth. All of these are waging war for valuable brain real estate with the important things I know that relate to my family life, business life and especially my spiritual life. So, while I viewed the number with some satisfaction, I was not sure it was entirely accurate.

Patterns

One thing that sparked my interest, though, was the accompanying assessment of my manner of thinking associated with the results of this test. The test's conclusion was that "mathematic analyst" described my predominate way of thinking. That's a fancy way of saying I have a mind for math (my best subject in school) which is aided by my ability to look for patterns in things, thereby assisting my comprehension abilities. Though I viewed the IQ score with some suspicion, I readily agreed this was the way I experienced my brain working in school, in the business world and in interpersonal relationships. The test had successfully applied a label to something I knew inherently and by experience about how my mind works best.

More importantly, because this is how God designed me, it's the way I approach studying the bible and more specifically the topic of discipleship. Ever since I started my teaching ministry more than 36 years ago, I have experienced a growing passion for studying and teaching how Christians develop to maturity in their walk with Christ (hence this book). As I pursued a more intentional study of this topic, I kept looking for a pattern to help me both understand and then convey to others this essential issue. After all, after salvation, we will spend the rest of our lives growing and maturing as a disciple (hopefully), so I felt it would be great to hit upon a way to remember the principles upon which we can mature in this area until they become organic in us.

It dawned on me, as a teacher, it might be helpful to adopt a mnemonic device of some sort to pass along to students helping them focus in an organized way on the main points of discipleship that could then serve as a springboard to delving into more detailed, related issues. After all, this approach is not without precedent in scripture. God commanded the Jews to include a memory device in their clothing. Take a look at Numbers 15:38-39:

> 38"*Speak to the Israelites and say to them: 'Throughout the generations to come you are to make tassels on the corners of your garments, with a blue cord on each tassel.* 39 *You will have these tassels to look at and* ***so you will remember all the commands of the Lord****, that you may obey them and not prostitute yourselves by chasing after the lusts of your own hearts and eyes".*

As I began to break down this monumental topic into its basic building blocks it became apparent to me that, at its foundation, there were five areas of discipleship that determine how we would grow to the maturity God intends.

Those five areas are:

- Following Jesus (and all that entails)
- Learning from Jesus
- Adhering to what He teaches us
- Imitating Jesus (conforming to His image)
- Replicating this growth in other disciples on that same narrow path

To remember this (and also the chronology involved, which I believe is of utmost importance), I settled on the memory device of an acronym, specifically the word "**FLAIR**" (the first letters of each of these five areas). In addition, the word flair has an interesting meaning which ties in well with the goal for a disciple.

The dictionary defines "flair" as "a special ability for doing something well". In addition, the word "flair" comes to us in the English from the Latin word *fragrare* meaning "sweet smell". It's where we get our English word "fragrance".

Paul, in describing gifts he received from a body of believers, characterized them in Philippians 4:18 this way:

> *"They are a fragrant offering, an acceptable sacrifice, pleasing to God."*

Or, check out this great verse in Ezekiel 20:41:

> *"I will accept you as fragrant incense when I bring you out from the nations and gather you from the countries where you have been scattered, and I will be proved holy through you in the sight of the nations."*

Or, do a key word search on the word "fragrance" in the Old Testament and most of them will be in Song of Songs which metaphorically describes our relationship with our Lord. I'll cover more of this in a later chapter.

PUTTING YOUR FLAIR IN MOTION

Have you ever done anything with a flair? Or do you have a flair for doing something? The New Collegiate Dictionary gives these two definitions for the word "flair":

- natural talent or aptitude
- instinctive discernment

I have owned and operated a printing and graphic design business for more than four decades. In that time, by virtue of the nature of my clientele, I have often been exposed to people who have a flair for design or a flair for using just the right color or crafting just the right phrase in their copywriting. Beyond the creative vocations, we see people with this type of innate talent in many walks of life.

What if we could develop that kind of reputation with regard to the way we lived as disciples of the Lord Jesus Christ? What if we were people with a flair for discipleship with a natural, organic way of living out our faith, coupled with an instinctive discernment of the ways in which God is working to sanctify us and set us apart for His purposes?

For the past twenty years or so, whenever I teach on the foundations of maturing as a disciple I have used this acronym as a pattern for our learning process and enticing my students with the title "A Flair for Discipleship". This 5-pronged view is what I will use in this book to help you understand the process of moving from a new, immature disciple to a mature, fruit-bearing disciple. Or if you are already farther along on the discipleship continuum, to help you efficiently proceed along the path to greater maturity.

The caution for me in this approach has been in avoiding anything that becomes overly formulaic or simply an exercise in methodology. Our interaction with the Holy Spirit is hard to pin down if your only approach is a methodology or checklist. However, I take great comfort in scriptural direction that points us to this very type of approach. Consider, for instance, Psalm 50, a psalm of Asaph. Specifically, in verse 23 is one of God's great promises:

> *The one who offers thanksgiving as his sacrifice glorifies me; to one who* ***orders his way rightly*** *I will show the salvation of God!"* Psalm 50:23 ESV

The emphasis there is mine to draw your attention to God's directive to put some order into the way we think and approach our narrow path journey. In viewing other translations besides the English Standard Version, the 1984 New International Version translates it "*prepares the way*", the New King James Version has it " *orders his ways aright*", and the New American Standard Bible "*sets his way properly*". You get the idea: this is a pointed instruction to recognize the pattern evident in the Word and then to assemble our life's journey so that it matches that pattern. The result of this ought to be an orderly, well thought-out approach to our participation as God sanctifies us and matures us.

A Lifetime Approach

The idea that we will spend all of the time (between our salvation experience and our death and glorification) being sanctified, is not as evident to many believers as we might hope. The blame for that lies in two areas. The first is the disheartening biblical illiteracy in much of the church. When we look at this through a historical perspective in America we are reminded that the bible originally was used as the primer to teach children reading at the founding of our country. Today any attempt to even reference the bible in schools is met with hostility or indifference. Because of this regression, this type of illiteracy in our culture is, unfortunately, to be expected.

In addition, many churches do not have an intentional discipleship growth mindset. Discipleship instruction in the Church generally occurs through bible studies and small groups but those are rarely attended by the majority of the members. Even at that, the question still lingers as to how intentional that teaching is toward an orderly way of growing as a disciple. Often this subject is taught with a scattershot approach, in hopes that something will hit the target. Hopefully, you'll find this book as a helpful guide to what a better approach can look like if you are not already experiencing it in your local church.

To illuminate this last point, consider Willowcreek Church in Illinois. A couple of decades ago they were the largest church in America, and by every measure a church that was immensely successful at preaching the gospel to the lost and shepherding them through their conversion into kingdom members. However, alarmingly, the Willowcreek staff came to the realization that they were not doing a good job at discipling these new believers. Despite the learned voices preaching from their pulpit, their vast physical and financial resources and the spiritual momentum derived from consistently seeing people coming to faith, they realized that they were successfully accomplishing only part of what the church is called to do.

The result was that Willowcreek embarked on a three year study, focusing primarily on surveying churches all over the world and finding out what was and what was not working with regard to helping believers grow to maturity in Christ. Out of that study came their published conclusions in a book entitled "*Reveal: Where Are You*" by Greg Hawkins and Cally Parkinson. It is an eye-opening work and I highly recommend it to anyone who is interested in a detailed discovery of how the Church can best assist the Holy Spirit in moving people of faith along the continuum of growing discipleship.

Overlapping, Cycling and Growing

Finally, and perhaps most importantly, as we move into the specific discussion of each of these five stages in the subsequent chapters, I want to point out a couple of characteristics about this process that are involved in moving through these stages.

First, let me point out there is no "end point" or "hard stop" to these stages in this lifetime. It is certainly meant to encompass our entire life in Christ from salvation to glorification. Those two events are the great bookends of our walk, whereby each is a one-time, work of God on our lives with eternal consequences. We contribute nothing to our salvation/justification and we contribute nothing to our eventual glorification. That is all the work of our sovereign Lord. However, the life in between those two instantaneous events is a long period of time where God calls us to partner with Him in our sanctification. He does the heavy lifting but we are (or should be) working in congress with Him for the purpose of attaining maturity as the Apostle Paul says in Ephesians 4:12b-13:

> [12]*"...so that the body of Christ may be built up* [13] *until we all reach unity in the faith and in the knowledge of the Son of God and* ***become mature, attaining to the whole measure of the fullness of Christ.****"*

Definitely there should not ever be a time in our lives when we say "we are done" or "I can stop now".

In addition, the nature of these five stages is that they exhibit an overlap. In other words, we don't come completely to the end of one before starting the next. Once we begin to follow, we begin to learn and even to obey. Adherence does not just start when we have first learned *everything*. Each stage will begin to bleed into the next to provide for a comfortable segue as we begin to master each of these five areas.

Finally. we don't go through this cycle just once and then we are done. In each area, we cycle back through. In other words, we continue to follow better and learn more, so we obey more and imitate Christ better and become more adept at making new disciples. Each cycle takes us closer and closer to that goal of "*the whole measure of the fullness of Christ*".

Perhaps I can express this last point best with a metaphor. Imagine that you have a desire to buy a sailboat and learn to be a sailor. You have grand designs on sailing across the ocean one day and you have now made that first boat purchase. You must then make a right assessment of where and how to proceed.

You should begin your journey not by launching out on your own but by first sailing with someone who is an expert, to begin to understand what it means to captain a boat from someone who already does it successfully. That leads to the process of learning about the boat, the riggings, what to do in different types of weather, how to tack and how to hoist the mainsail.

Eventually you get to lay your hand to the tiller and begin to put into practice the things you have learned from your captain, and hopefully with much practice, your abilities begin to mimic his. Only then do you have the abilities and confidence to then invite others aboard your own boat when you take the helm.

This is essentially what we are doing in this five-fold process on our disciple journey. But, like this new captain, we want to continue to grow in our understanding of greater sailing adventures and put in place practices that enable you to handle more difficult journeys. Ultimately we grow in our ability to not only take on more passengers but we also become equipped to train other new sailors who desire the same challenges you have mastered.

This is the continuing process of growing to maturity as a disciple that we find in this process of ordering our ways rightly. Now, let's take a look at the first one: following.

Questions for Discussion

What are the inherent strengths to having a mnemonic device to help you understand better the things involved in your growth?

How beneficial is it to your walk to consider that the bible promotes an orderliness and purpose for our growth??

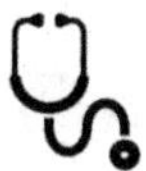

Which of the five elements of this discipleship process do you consider to be the most difficult or confusing?

Chapter Six

"The only thing Christianity cannot be is moderately important."

–C.S. Lewis

Following Jesus

A survey by the George Barna Group over 15 years ago found that 81% of born-again Christians stated that "*having a growing relationship with Jesus Christ is a top priority*". That same survey found that 47% of non-Christians said the same thing!

There are a couple of things to derive from analyzing this data. First, we might naturally wonder what was up with the 19% of born-again believers who did not answer yes to this question. Are they already there or do they simply not understand the importance of a growing relationship with Jesus? Second, it tells us that there are many unbelievers who would readily and eagerly become Christians if we just shared the gospel with them and helped them understand. That is the good news of this survey.

Now, look around you. Are the vast majority of Christians you see living a true discipleship relationship where Jesus Christ is obviously number one in their lives? Here is where the survey cannot give us enough information, and that's the not-so-good news. A survey like this cannot always distinguish between deeply held beliefs and answers that sound like what the surveyor wants to hear. But if your own observation of other believers does not reveal that there is an overwhelming success in this area, then that 81% figure could be some who are successfully growing in their walk and others who are simply recognizing the importance but doing little about it. Or, more likely, they desire it but don't know how to get there (and that is what this series of lessons is about).

If we were to take, for instance, formal group bible study as just one measuring stick for whether or not someone is seriously pursuing this type of growing relationship, then we would have to disqualify most people in a couple of major denominations, which rarely even emphasize that type of corporate study.

In fact, in the church I attend, we have a minority of our folks involved in this type of group study. Of course, I know I may be preaching to the choir here a bit and those small numbers are not necessarily the result of a church inadequately promoting the importance of formal bible study. The responsibility for undesirable levels of bible study attendance ultimately rests on those who are not availing themselves of the proffered study opportunities.

The "why not" aspect of this problem keeps spiritual formation experts awake at night wondering what type of studies would attract more students. Or, more to the point: why don't more Christians experience a greater hunger for studying God's Word?

Group bible study is surely not the only way we can place the highest priority on our growth in Christ. What this survey should tell us, combined with our own observation, is that we (the Church) have a problem. The Church universal has too many people who call themselves believers but define "following Jesus" as 90 minutes of semi-regular church attendance and an occasional gratuitous offering. Recently in my own denomination we saw headlines that indicated Southern Baptists were going the wrong direction in almost every key metric, while those self-identifying as "unaffiliated" keep increasing. If the transformation that accompanies maturing as a disciple is not being made the top priority by born-again believers, then we have a problem with people rightly following Jesus Christ. This short circuits the prospect of becoming true disciples from the very start.

My sense is that the best approach to turning this issue around is to take an organized and orderly approach to learning what it means to become a mature disciple and how to grow toward that goal. It starts with step one in our first look at the five identifiable aspects of the disciple's life.

As a reminder, those five areas are:

- Following Jesus (and all that entails)

- Learning from Jesus
- Adhering to what He teaches us
- Imitating Jesus (conforming to His image)
- Replicating this growth in other disciples on that same narrow path

To remember this (and also the chronology involved which I believe is of utmost importance), let me remind you I am using the acronym **FLAIR** (the first letters of each of the above five areas) and this chapter's lesson will be on the first element: *following Jesus*.

Difficulty with the Idea of Following

If you were asked why Christians have a problem following Jesus the way He intends, you could undoubtedly come up with numerous answers. At the core of the issue is the vernacular that is different between the first century and the 21st. If we lived during the roughly thousand days of Jesus' earthly ministry, and we were asked if we followed Jesus, there would be a part of that answer that reflected a geographic component. A dictionary definition of the word "follow" shows the primary meaning to be *"go or come after (a person or thing proceeding ahead); move or travel behind"*.

It's a proximity issue.

If we were followers of Jesus in the first century, we would have spent at least some time actually going to hear Him speak, being eye witnesses to His miracles, and maybe even following Him around from one place to another. We see that in passages like Mark 10:52 where Jesus has just given a blind man sight:

> *"Go," said Jesus, "your faith has healed you." Immediately he received his sight and* ***followed Jesus along the road****."*

Not so in the 21st century. Now, following takes on a different perspective. The question about the problem of following Jesus, then, no longer involves what physical road we walk with Jesus, but instead involves a more complex answer. At the root of that answer is simply the need to break through with a full understanding of what following Jesus entails. It should be obvious that when Jesus gave instructions to "*follow Me*" he meant more than giving traveling directions to those traipsing along behind Him as He moved about Judea. And He means more than that today.

In our time, the first place we encounter this question of "a correct perspective on following" is at the beginning stage when a believer makes a decision to follow Christ. Often it is in response to an altar call, perhaps to a song like *"I Have Decided to Follow Jesus"*, which is sung in countless churches across this world. There is no telling how many people have responded to this or a similar song of appeal as they said "yes" to God's invitation in the gospel. And yet, we all come into the faith without a full understanding of the cost and surrender that is involved, and certainly have little clarity yet about the challenges ahead on the narrow path. Interestingly, tradition has this great hymn mentioned above being the final words of a martyred Indian who had converted to Christianity shortly before he and his family were murdered in the middle of the 19th century. He certainly understood the cost, but most of us, responding to this great hymn or one like it, in that moment do not have a full appreciation of the cost. That is why Jesus found it necessary, multiple times, to talk about the requisite costs with such terms as:

- deny yourself (Luke 9:23)
- take up your cross (Luke 9:23)
- let the dead bury their own dead (Matthew 8:22)
- lay aside excuses about your field, your new oxen, even your marriage (Luke 14: 18-20)
- hate your parents, family, siblings and even your own life in order to follow as a disciple (Luke 14:26)

Those are jolting to hear at the beginning of your faith journey, even more so here as we see them without their full context. Perhaps it's why Jesus took three years to drill these things into his disciples who followed him daily. And to be fair, Jesus does not expect us to have a mature understanding of these things in the beginning. But He does not expect us to ignore them either as we begin to be sanctified.

The starting point for how we begin to take in these complex, hard-hitting teachings begins with learning to follow Christ properly in full surrender. And the natural question that follows that statement is one that must be dealt with by every sheep coming into the Great Shepherd's flock. *How do I rightly follow Jesus?*

Often, when I am contending with the challenge of discovering what a difficult statement means, I start by filtering out the more obvious things that it **does not** mean. In 2025, where there is a problem with following Jesus properly, I believe the answer to the "problem" is one of three possibilities of what following *does not* mean.

Following Wrongly

Sometimes people follow the wrong thing or person. The bible is full of examples showing that people are, by nature, followers, but often make a dangerously poor decision on who to follow, or they pick someone who is right to follow, but follow incompletely or incorrectly. Or, they just don't understand the ramifications of true following. The bible gives these examples of people who were followed, showing how confused some have become:

a. Jesus (77 times in Gospels)
b. Paul
c. Apollos
d. Cephas
e. Balaam
f. Judas the Galilean
g. Satan
h. deceiving spirits
i. sheep following a shepherd

j. angels (Peter)
k. Theudas
l. self (flesh, evil)- many references

Consider those who followed cult leader Sun Yung Moon, for example. His teachings referenced God, Jesus, and cherry-picked bible verses, but he spent most of the time touting his own teaching of enlightenment, mixed with plain old fashion heresy. He claimed to be a messiah and authored sacred texts that he blended with biblical texts that produced an amalgam theology, corrupt at its core. Despite growing up in a North Korean family that had converted to Christianity when he was a child, he was a false teacher.

Yet some heard Sun Yung Moon talk about Jesus and thought they could follow Jesus by following him. Mormons and Jehovah's Witnesses teach theology that is equally problematic because their following Jesus demands the mixing of theology that is true with that which is untrue.

Following Multiple Targets

Often people want to follow two things, hoping each satisfies different parts of us, but in reality are mutually exclusive. Such a problem can be seen when we observe the polar opposites of Christianity and humanism. Christianity declares we are created to glorify God; to serve God; for His good purpose; to have a relationship with God.

Humanism, on the other hand, says man is the master of his own fate or destiny; man establishes moral values; man is essentially good on his own merit.

To break down humanism even further we see:

- existentialism: Everything is permitted; freedom is the foundation of all his values
- relativism: no absolute truth; no standards
- materialism: physical well-being and worldly possessions constitute the highest value and greatest good

When you see these definitions, consider how many people around us exhibit characteristics in keeping with these humanist approaches. Christianity and humanism are clearly opposites, one antithetical to the other. However, to introduce yet another *"ism"* term, syncretism occurs when there is an attempt to straddle the two. It produces cultural Christians or carnal Christians. Take a peek at 1 Cor 3:1-3 where Paul decries Christians who have tried to mix elements of Christianity with something else that is incompatible.

> [1] *"Brothers and sisters, I could not address you as people who live by the Spirit but as people who are still worldly—mere infants in Christ.* [2] *I gave you milk, not solid food, for you were not yet ready for it. Indeed, you are still not ready.* [3] *You are still worldly. For since there is jealousy and quarreling among you, are you not worldly? Are you not acting like mere humans?"*

Who would have ever thought the term "mere humans" could be used as such an insult? But Paul uses it that way to describe believers who have not begun to progress along the path of discipleship but have instead continued to keep one foot firmly planted in the world. This syncretism is the attempt to merge two life views into one. God won't stand for this, as He declares through His prophet in 1st Kings 18:21:

> *"Elijah went before the people and said, "How long will you waver between two opinions? If the LORD is God, follow him; but if Baal is God, follow him." But the people said nothing."*

A good part of the story of Solomon serves as the cautionary tale of someone who ended up trying to blend God's ways and man's ways. Here is what God said of Solomon in 1st Kings 11:6:

> *"So Solomon did evil in the eyes of the LORD; he did not follow the LORD completely, as David his father had done".*

Lack of Real Understanding of Following

Finally we come to the option where people don't fully understand what is necessary to follow. This is the third possible answer, and where the first two can be resolved by reduction (reducing who we follow, to Christ alone, and reducing our allegiance to Christianity alone), this third possibility involves expanding our understanding of the fullness of Jesus' teachings.

Hopefully, it is obvious why we must first tackle the issue of "correct" following. Without an accurate picture of what this entails, there is no proper foundation for learning from Jesus, adhering to what He has taught, imitating Christ, and certainly, we are in a poor position of replicating ourselves in others. Or more accurately, we are in danger of making more weak, problem-prone disciples.

❧

I hope you took note of the way I phrased "learning" above. It would be incorrect to state that there is no learning whatsoever involved in how we begin to follow Jesus. He does not come to us as an unknown entity and demand blind faith. The distinction here is that in this first stage, we learn *"of"* Jesus and that He desires that we follow Him, which assists us in making the commitment necessary to do just that. We learn *of* Him from reading, observing, hearing. Some learn via more dramatic ways like dreams and visions and other ways in which our Lord desires to reveal Himself to the faithless. But we must commit to follow Him before we can begin stage two, which is to learn *"from"* Him.

Battling Culture's Take on Following

In our day, the thing that complicates matters is that there is clearly a problem with the cultural understanding of what it means to "follow". Consider a popular contemporary cultural idea of following: "*to follow someone on 'X' (formerly Twitter)*". Now think about the results of that bizarre type of following. We peek in from time to time when it is convenient. We most often limit our involvement in sharing the wisdom of the one we follow to "reposts" and "likes". We make brevity in our own participation (a limited number of characters) our standard which puts us in the habit of brief, anonymous encounters with people instead of long, close relationships. Consider how these same type of culturally ingrained "following" habits diminish our ability to follow Jesus as He desires, if these characteristics similarly describe how we follow Him.

Just as important as it was in the first century, Jesus still beckons people to follow Him today, just as He did 2,000 years ago when He walked this earth with His disciples. But again, it is clear that "follow" doesn't just mean to physically trail behind. There is much more to it. The Greek word for "follow" used in the New Testament is *akoloutheo* which means literally "a like way". It typically signifies companionship, in that it speaks to people going in a like way. It becomes more the manner in which we live that reflects Christ, not the geography of where we are walking.

Viewing the passages in the gospels that deal with those who followed Jesus gives us insight into an important evaluative method for step one of understanding better how to follow Jesus. By looking at the examples of three groups, we can set up a filter for determining where we are as well as discern another difference between sheep and disciples. We do this by looking at their motivations.

THREE TYPES OF FOLLOWERS

Crowds followed Jesus to get what they wanted (there are no skills associated with this type of following, it is just motivated by self-gratification). Sometimes there was some intentionality involved, as when people sought Jesus out at the Sermon on the Mount or other locations. Often, the crowds just happened to be out and about in areas where Jesus determined to speak, such as the Temple courts and the synagogues. The crowds wanted healing (Luke 5:15), they wanted signs and miracles (Luke 11:29), and they wanted teaching (Mark 2:13).

Sheep, on the other hand, follow to get what they deserve and what they need. Their essential skill is Voice Recognition (see John 10:3-5 where John describes how the sheep know the Master's voice):

> [3] *The gatekeeper opens the gate for him, and the sheep listen to his voice. He calls his own sheep by name and leads them out.* [4] *When he has brought out all his own, he goes on ahead of them, and his sheep follow him because they know his voice.* [5] *But they will never follow a stranger; in fact, they will run away from him because they do not recognize a stranger's voice."*

Disciples, though, follow in order to learn and to do and to serve. Observation becomes an essential skill here. Matthew 9:35-36 shows how Jesus modeled behavior for the disciples in hope that they would begin to learn by diligently observing Him at work.

> *[35] Jesus went through all the towns and villages, teaching in their synagogues, proclaiming the good news of the kingdom and healing every disease and sickness. [36] When he saw the crowds, he had compassion on them, because they were harassed and helpless, like sheep without a shepherd.*

Re-Thinking Following

I was six years old in 1961 when John Kennedy was inaugurated as our 35th president. It was the first time I can remember being aware of anything political. One of the most memorable things I heard during this time of my new awareness was a famous line from Kennedy's inaugural address that year: "*Ask not what your country can do for you...ask what you can do for your country*". It's probably the most well know of his quotes, despite the fact it was probably penned by a speech writer. What is significant about it in the context of this discussion is that sometimes, even unintentionally in political discussions, an idea emerges that has its roots in the kingdom.

Following Jesus first requires a change in our way of thinking that matches this idea. This may be the first truly revolutionary thing to change in how we determine the worth of this lifelong journey toward discipleship maturity. We begin to change our motivation from *"what can He provide us"* to *"what can I do for Him"*. We see Jesus clueing us in on this in Matthew 6:33.

> *"But seek first his kingdom and his righteousness, and all these things will be given to you as well."*

This is not the only place we see this, though. Paul makes this statement at the beginning of chapter 12 of the book of Romans, verse 2, a short passage that is built upon everything Paul has taught in chapters 1-11. This is a true Romans 12:2 notion:

> *"Do not conform any longer to the pattern of this world, but be transformed by the renewing of your mind".*

We have to rethink the whole idea of following Jesus. For the disciple, following is not just salvation to us today anymore than following was only being healed in Jesus' day. Healing was, at that time, certainly a precursor to following and a necessary way in which Christ reached people. Similarly, Jesus makes followers out of those He saves.

Consequently, there are ways we must prepare ourselves for what following demands. Jesus said it like this in Matthew 16:24:

> *"Then Jesus said to his disciples, "If anyone would come after me, he must deny himself and take up his cross and follow me."* [Luke's parallel passage adds the word "daily" to taking up our cross.]

Jesus is telling us to "spend your life, do not hoard it". He tells us that using two of the most eye-opening commands in the bible.

DENY YOURSELF

In Matthew 18:3, Jesus articulated it this way:

> "*And he said: "I tell you the truth, unless you change and become like little children, you will never enter the kingdom of heaven. Therefore, whoever humbles himself like this child is the greatest in the kingdom of heaven*".

Jesus told the disciples that denying yourself means to humble yourself, and He used the example of a little child to drive home His point. On the contrary, cult leaders will tell you that, like any good parent, God supposedly wants His children to grow up to be greater than Him. The heretical false teacher tells you to exalt yourself. Jesus links following Him to humbling yourself. This must be our initial step.

We can take a hint at what this phrase means by looking at Peter when he denied Christ. After Christ's arrest, he said of Jesus "*I do not know this Man*". While that statement was uttered aloud at that moment out of panic and fear, I believe Peter ultimately came to understand those same words more clearly when directed inwardly. Denying yourself means to no longer reckon yourself as important and no longer consider "self" as the most important thing that exists. In other words, humbling ourselves as a believer means we no longer seek to know the man (or woman) we once were before we became a Christ-follower.

Take up your cross daily

Examining this command, it's obvious the disciples did not understand that Jesus was going to be crucified. However, because they lived under Roman rule, they understood the sacrificial nature of what Jesus was describing. The Romans were involved in crucifixion from the 6th Century BC to the 3rd Century AD when Constantine put an end to it (the Romans did not invent crucifixion, they just perfected it; in fact, crucifixion originated in the Chaldean days). Some have estimated the Romans crucified over a million and a half people. That's an average of four people crucified every day for almost a thousand years. It's unimaginable in its horror and magnitude. The disciples had undoubtedly witnessed plenty of crucifixions and knew what the cross was a symbol for: death and a terrible one at that (the English word "excruciating" comes from the Greek word for crucifixion).

Jesus was exhorting them to a life that included the burden of sacrificial living and service, as well as the possibility of excruciating episodes, in response to their life of faith. It's a focus on counting the costs of following Jesus. Consider this: when we get married, the pastor says *"Marriage is not something entered into lightly."* So much more this companionship/commitment with Jesus.

What does this following look like for those of us who have said *"Yes"* to the call to live "in a like way", to change our way of thinking and to live a life that points outward more than it points inward? Here are some examples that get us on the right path.

What we must do

- *"let the dead bury the dead"*: give up even the seemingly good things for the better things
- Using the example of the rich young man in Luke 18:18 whom Jesus counseled to sell everything and give to poor: give up things that are misplaced priorities and cloud our real purpose in following Jesus

What we must become

- Fishers of men: focused on bringing people into the kingdom (focus on people rather than things, prestige, accomplishments)
- Instead of being served, become servants.

> *"Whoever serves me must follow me; and where I am, my servant also will be. My Father will honor the one who serves me." (John 12:26).*

- We must be focused on serving those who have come into the kingdom. This verse above, by the way, is a great example of an important precept: A command is a promise! God's commands always come coupled with a promise of blessing for those who obey.

What we must avoid

- The rich young man also reminds us of another connection.

After the young man expressed his desire to follow in the most comfortable way, it says in verse 24 that Jesus "looked" at him. It is one of two places where Jesus is said, in the original language, to have literally "looked with love" at someone. In both cases, it is someone who follows improperly.

- Peter made the critical error of following Jesus improperly after His arrest, by "following Him from a distance". This elicited the same "looking with love" response from Jesus. However, for Peter it led to denial, remembering words too late, remorse, and bitter weeping. Indeed, the quickest way to make a mess of things is to follow Jesus from a distance.

Perspective

Perspective is an interesting concept and in the question of how to properly follow Christ, it is everything. Whether it is a self-evaluation of how we are following the wrong thing, trying to follow two things simultaneously, or just flat out not understanding what following in the 21st century entails, the thing that is required in order to begin to follow the correct way is a change in perspective. We must first begin to adopt the perspective of God's word rather than the perspective of the culture of the self. By doing this we begin to lay a solid foundation for how we learn, adhere, imitate and ultimately replicate our maturity in others.

Also when we do this, we accomplish what is perhaps the greatest indicator of following Jesus in this new perspective, and that is accepting His authority over all of our life. This is the very essence of being able to call Him "Lord".

Questions for Discussion

What characteristics of a child so impressed Jesus that He used that to teach humility to His disciples?

What new truth was illuminated in this last chapter?

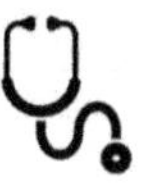

As you consider following Jesus in the 21st century, what do you think needs to change to bring your following in line with Jesus' expectations?

Chapter Seven

"When one teaches, two learn."

–Robert Heinlein

Learning From Jesus

I have a friend (also a business client) who was, among other things, an award-winning news broadcast journalist on our local CBS affiliate back in the 1980's. For the last 25 years or so, she has been teaching communication and leadership strategies through her own consulting business. One of the by-products of doing business with her, for me, has been the opportunity to read and learn from many of the materials we have been reproducing for her over the years. Because of that, I have gained insight I might not otherwise have into communication methods, as well as with a subject that is joined at the hip to communications: learning.

Simply stated, the goal of communications can be boiled down to learning, and the goal of learning is to understand what is being communicated. Of course, the processes involved can be quite complex. It is essential that we employ good methods of learning if we are going to understand what God is communicating to us regarding the topic of discipleship.

To illustrate the difficulty factor that can be involved in learning the Word, let me share something I read on my friend's website a while back on *The Power of Body Language*. A lot of the information was geared toward business meetings and speaking engagements, but the part that caught my eye was the following:

"Studies have found that:

- *ONLY 7% of communication comes from the words you say*
- *38% comes from vocal elements (tone, speed, inflections)*
- *55% comes from non-verbal communication (facial expressions, posture, gestures)"*

As you might imagine, the disciples and the crowds that followed Jesus may have had a leg up on us simply by virtue of seeing His expressions, hearing the inflection in His voice and observing His hand gestures, not to mention being eyewitnesses to miracles and supernatural events. So how do we, as people separated by nearly 2,000 years from the time Christ taught on this earth, learn when we have the disadvantage of not having been in Jesus' presence? Can we expect to learn all we need to in order to grow into the type of mature disciples that reflect the very heart of our Savior? Is there a way to learn that we might not be taking advantage of?

I am glad you asked! The answer is "yes". For one thing, by reading this material you are involved in the process right now in a way that was unavailable to people in Jesus' time. Also, you are likely a member or visitor of a local church body and hopefully have learned more there. Perhaps today you'll pick up the bible or an inspirational book and undoubtedly learn even more. But, the purpose of this chapter is to get us to think a little bit differently about the process of learning, partly by examining examples in the biblical text about learning, and possibly by modifying our - there's that word again - *"perspective"* on the subject a bit.

This chapter is our look at the second of the five identifiable aspects of the disciple's life. As I mentioned in the previous chapter, these five areas of discipleship determine how we can develop into the mature disciples God intends us to become. As a reminder, those five areas are:

- Following Jesus (and all that entails)
- Learning from Jesus
- Adhering to what He teaches us
- Imitating Jesus (conforming to His image)
- Replicating this growth in other disciples on that same narrow path

To remember this (and also the chronology involved which I believe is of utmost importance), I'll remind you again I am using the acronym **FLAIR** (the first letters of each of the above five areas) and this chapter will cover the second element: *learning from Jesus*.

Since this chapter title is *"Learning from Jesus"*, let's begin with an important aspect about Christ that we might not always readily associate with the usual way we learn. In John 8:12, we see John informing us of one the most important distinctions that Jesus ever made about Himself.

> *"When Jesus spoke again to the people, he said, "I am the light of the world. Whoever follows me will never walk in darkness, but will have the light of life."*

The background here is the Feast of Tabernacles with the giant menorah in the middle of the Court of the Women of the temple, reminding the Jews of the fire that led them in the wilderness. I took a photo when I was in Jerusalem a few years ago of a similar menorah which was recreated for the first time since the destruction of the second temple, and stands ready to be employed again when the temple is rebuilt. It is immense and gives you an idea of how that menorah could have cast light over a very large area of the city.

Against this backdrop Jesus publicly proclaimed that He is the Light of the World. This "light" has a clear salvation ring to it. However, there are discipleship elements that are important as we look at the concept of "light" and understand why Jesus selected that as the simile for His task to the world.

Light makes things accessible. Think of spelunkers, those brave, slightly crazy adventurers who find that their greatest high is crawling around in dark caves. But, the interior of a cave is inaccessible without light.

> *God, the blessed and only Ruler, the King of kings and Lord of lords, who alone is immortal and who lives in unapproachable light, whom no one has seen or can see. To him be honor and might forever. Amen. (1 Timothy 6:15-16).*

The modifier here means both unapproachable and inaccessible. Jesus makes God accessible to us just as a flashlight makes the inner contours of a dark cave accessible.

Light brings everything to a superlative level. The speed of light is the fastest speed (quantum physicists may debate this); gamma ray bursts generated by quasars (a form of light) are the most powerful forces in the universe; white light has all the colors; light defies physical laws (it can be both wave and a particle). And, everything about Christ, as the Light-provider is equally remarkable and unparalleled.

Light is an illuminator. It opens up our eyes to knowledge. This is perhaps the most obvious learning characteristic associated with light.

Light is the "discernment-enabler". Expanding on the above, it is only by virtue of light that we can discern details like form and color (try telling a green apple from a red one in a darkened room). These last two points help us experience transition from disciples as followers to disciples as learners.

Learning's Aim

A critical aspect of the learning process is the target of our searching. Obviously, we seek the truth. This is why the disciples followed Jesus, so that they could observe The Truth making known the truth.

Like those first disciples, we must recognize the truth as a powerful ally of growth as well as our liberator from the many non-truths that compete for our attention. In the previous passage in John, Jesus follows up with a declaration of the Truth:

> *"To the Jews who had believed him, Jesus said, "If you hold to my teaching, you are really my disciples. Then you will know the truth, and the truth will set you free."* (John 8:31-32)

How important was the truth to Jesus? In John's gospel alone, Jesus makes twenty-six statements that He begins with the phrase *"I tell you the truth"*. That many mentions by our Lord must garner our attention. The word He uses for *"the truth"* has already captured much of your attention, and you may not even be aware of it. The phrase *"the truth"* is translated from the Hebrew word *ameyn*. The Greek transliteration of that word is "*amen*".

Look familiar? Of course, we close all our prayers with that word, and when we do, we are saying to God that the prayers from our heart and on our lips represent the truth to us. Jesus used it as a way to draw attention at the front end of His statements, to alert His listeners that what would follow would be the truth from His heart.

By emphasizing the phrase *"know the truth"* Jesus is pointing out the difference between being aware that a truth exists versus learning it. An example: I am aware that airplanes fly. I am aware of that truth. But until I learn about Bernoulli's principle (as the speed of moving air or water increases, the pressure within the fluid decreases) I cannot know *how* it can fly and I don't know how to *make* something stay aloft.

Consider how many times as parents we are left with the answer "just because" to our kids because we are stumped at a question. Is that a satisfactory answer when someone asks a spiritual question of us that has eternal consequences? Of course not, and that is why we aren't just accumulating spiritual facts but instead have the goal of learning the significance and the application of the truths that we discover on this narrow path.

Why Learn

There are other reasons why we must learn. In fact, while there are at least 15 scriptural reasons, here are three that are especially important to maturing disciples:

First, God has trusted us with His message. Paul writes in 1st Thessalonians 2:4:

"We speak as men approved by God to be entrusted with the

gospel."

If you entrusted me with your money to invest in the stock market you would have a concern that I had learned or would learn how best to do that. Likewise, God expects those, into whom He has placed His highest trust, to be certain they have learned how to make the best use of the gospel.

Second, a disciple's life has need of hope. At a later date, Paul writes in Romans 14:5:

> *"For everything that was written in the past was written to teach us, so that through endurance and the encouragement of the Scriptures we might have hope."*

Here we begin to see the major avenue through which we gain the hope necessary to propel us in ministry and even deeper learning.

Finally, in our ministry as disciples, as in all areas of our life, we covet God's gracious blessings. In the Old Testament, Ezra was a priest, a scribe and a leader, who was in charge of the second group of Jewish exiles who returned to the Promised Land after their captivity in Babylon. To discover Ezra's impact on our goal for learning, we need to pick up his story in Ezra, chapter 7. Note the beginning description of the prophet Ezra in verses 6-10.

> *"After these things, during the reign of Artaxerxes king of Persia, Ezra son of Seraiah...—[6] this Ezra came up from Babylon. He was a teacher well versed in the Law of Moses, which the Lord, the God of Israel, had given. The king had granted him everything he asked, for the hand of the Lord his God was on him. [7] Some of the Israelites, including priests, Levites, musicians, gatekeepers and temple servants, also came up to Jerusalem in the seventh year of King Artaxerxes. [8] Ezra arrived in Jerusalem in the fifth month of the seventh year of the king. [9] He had begun his journey from Babylon on the first day of the first month, and he arrived in Jerusalem on the first day of the fifth month, for the gracious hand of his God was on him. [10] For Ezra had devoted himself to the study and observance of the Law of the Lord, and to teaching its decrees and laws in Israel."*

The Lord's hand was upon Him and enabled him to do that to which he was called. The reason: Ezra had devoted himself to the learning and obedience of the Law of the Lord, and to teaching those things he was learning and living. That kind of devotion is essential to the maturing disciple.

- Ezra received blessings from the king (v. 6)
- Ezra had the hand of the Lord God upon him (v. 9)
- Ezra took courage because the Lord's favor was upon him (v. 28)
- All this because Ezra did 4 very important things:

A Deeper View of the Example of Ezra

Ezra devoted himself. The first of these four important things

Ezra did is highlighted by the Hebrew word in the passage for "devoted' which means literally *"to stand up"*. The King James Version says he *"prepared himself"*. What he did was to take a stand. When others around us are "keeping their options open" we must take a stand and establish ourselves as devoted students of the Word. What we are doing when we state and follow through on our devotion is establishing a habit.

Interestingly enough, in Hebrews 5:8, the same was said of Jesus.

> *"Although he was a son, he* ***learned*** *obedience from what he suffered..."*

The utter importance of learning is illustrated by the model of our Lord who Himself "learned" obedience (this may sound puzzling for God in the flesh). The Greek for "learned" here is *manthano* which is a word that is connected with the word for "disciple". It has an interesting meaning here of "*acquired the habit of*". This speaks well of disciples that our learning process is geared toward our being habitually obedient (recall that maturing disciples do by reflex what they once did out of duty or discipline).

Ezra studied. The KJV says he "prepared himself to seek". Notice that he did not say he prepared himself to "notice" but rather to take a proactive stance and "study".

Ezra obeyed what he learned. We'll look at that in more depth in the next chapter when we talk about "Adhering".

Ezra taught what he learned to others. We have that same command (see the Great Commission). Whatever level of Christianity you find yourself in, you should teach others what you know. If all you know is Christ and Him crucified, teach that. I'll talk about this idea more in a later chapter on Replicating yourself in others.

Sources and Methods

If you have spent any time in the early 2020's following the political issues related to the US Intelligence Community, you have undoubtedly heard the phrase "sources and methods" a number of times. As important as they are in intelligence work, they are even more important to the learning disciple. We have talked about the Source, now let's spend a little time on methods.

The study of the subject of "learning" is quite extensive, and much of it relates to intellect and much to experience or behavior. But for the purpose of this chapter, let's agree to just break them down into **passive learning** and **active learning**. Both are beneficial methods for learning and have their place in how our brains take in, process and make use of outside information. The most extreme form of passive learning would be subliminal learning, where we learn with no real effort and may not even be aware we are in a learning mode. Many years ago a large department store began to play an advertising message in a subtrack under the background music being played in their elevators. The message was "buy more Coca Cola". Their Coca Cola sales went up 38% (that type of subliminal advertising has since been outlawed).

We employ a less extreme method of passive learning every time we sit and listen to a sermon (though the act of going to church to listen has an active component).

More common, passive learning can be something like I experienced one summer doing yardwork. I was weedeating around some liriope and got a little too close. It was then that I learned passively that this liriope plant was the home to a hidden squad of riled up yellow jackets. I also learned that they will chase you quite a ways and that, once attached to you, unlike their honeybee brethren, they will continue to sting you until they get bored or you squash them to dust. After downing a couple of anti-histamine tablets, I switched into active learning mode and began to seek out the wisdom available at my nearby hardware store where I spent some time educating myself on the best yellow jacket killer on the market. Or, I could have, once again, taken on the role of active learner by checking out YouTube on "How to Quickly Eliminate 1,000 Angry Yellowjackets in Just Minutes".

At this point, I have friends who may be reading this who are laughing at my ordeal. But what is the point of that story, other than to tickle their funny bone? It's to point out and ingrain the importance and necessity of the mode of *active* learner.

The first precept about a disciple's learning habits that leads to maturity is that, more and more, they become active, not passive. Our journey with Christ may begin passively, listening to pastors and teachers, but real maturity is gained when we get active. The Greek word that is translated "disciple" in the bible, *mathetes*, literally means *"a learner"*.

Endeavor

However, a look at the root of that word gives us a fuller, more insightful meaning: ***"thought accompanied by endeavor"***. This reference to our endeavor puts both the effort and the responsibility for learning more so on the pupil rather than the teacher. Like Ezra, any good teacher has a responsibility to study, incorporate what they learn into how they live, and then teach others likewise. The disciple has the responsibility for making every effort to receive the teaching, understand it, and live it.

Further, the word "*endeavor*" compels us more and more into the active realm. Here are some specifics about our active learning that can help us understand how this is best accomplished.

We must "go to Jesus" (directly in His word in our century).

> *"Now when he saw the crowds, he went up on a mountainside and sat down. His disciples came to him, and he began to teach them."* (Matthew 5:1-2)

Notice Jesus' focus on teaching His disciples as well as being the only source of that teaching.

> *"With many similar parables Jesus spoke the word to them, as much as they could understand. He did not say anything to them without using a parable. But when he was alone with his own disciples, he explained everything." (Mark 4:33-34)*

This wasn't a "*read chapters 1 and 2, there will be a test on Tuesday*" approach. Jesus was interested in teaching the truth and explaining it as well. By His Spirit, Jesus will reveal truth to us. It is not God's intent to keep understanding from us when we come to Him to learn.

Removing Distractions

Mary and Martha give us a good lesson on handling distractions that can impede our learning.

> *[38] "As Jesus and his disciples were on their way, he came to a village where a woman named Martha opened her home to him. [39] She had a sister called Mary, who sat at the Lord's feet listening to what he said. [40] But Martha was distracted by all the preparations that had to be made. She came to him and asked, "Lord, don't you care that my sister has left me to do the work by myself? Tell her to help me!" [41] "Martha, Martha," the Lord answered, "you are worried and upset about many things, but few things are needed. Mary has chosen what is better, and it will not be taken away from her." (Luke 10:38-42)*

Consider this: both sisters were attempting to sit at Jesus' feet and learn, but Martha allowed other things (even good things) to distract her. Those distractions typically give rise to "worry". The Greek word here literally means *"divided in mind"*. When we make an endeavor to study and learn from God's Word, we must have a focused mind, by removing distractions so that Jesus has our undivided attention.

Knowledge Compared With Understanding

We should endeavor to learn the "why's" and "how's" rather than just the "what's". After Jesus taught the crowds using the parable of the four soils, the disciples came to him (Matthew 13:10) and asked the following:

> *"Why do you speak to the people in parables?"*

They wanted to understand Jesus' methodology as much as the content of His teaching. This is critical for disciples concerned about their own ministry work. It's also critical because there are responsibilities that accompany learning. We see this later in Matthew 13:51-52 when, immediately after Jesus' teaching to the disciples of the seven parables of the kingdom, we read:

> *"Have you understood all these things?" Jesus asked. Yes," they replied. He said to them, "Therefore every teacher of the law who has been instructed about the kingdom of heaven is like the owner of a house who brings out of his storeroom new treasures as well as old."* (Matthew 13:51-52)

The phrase *"who has been instructed"* literally means *"who has been made a disciple"*. That's us. And, it's our responsibility to take the treasure we have learned and convey it to others. We are to share what we have learned.

We do this best by recognizing what God is revealing, using best methods to determine the interpretation of what is revealed, and then making every effort to personalize the teaching by seeking the area of appropriate application of what has been revealed and interpreted.

Or, a simpler way to say all that is expressed in three questions we can ask about anything we are studying:

What does it say? (Revelation)

What does it mean? (Interpretation)

What does it mean to me? (Application)

Once we become skilled at this type of learning, the application stage leads us into the next element of our discipleship growth: adhering to what we have learned.

Questions for Discussion

What is the most important thing you read about the learning process here that can make an impact on how you gain understanding of Jesus' teachings?

What new truth was illuminated in this last chapter?

At this point in your discipleship journey, would you describe your learning type more passive or active?

Chapter Eight

"The Cross...is the lighthouse set on the rocks of sin to warn you that swift and sure destruction awaits you if you continue to rebel against the Lord."

–C.H. Spurgeon

Adherence

I used to be a skeptic. No, not about salvation or the bible or the importance of the Church. I was a skeptic about chiropractic care. I can remember as a young man my mother regaling me with her stories of the benefits of her trips to the chiropractor and I remember, equally as well, thinking "hokey science, voodoo medicine". Like many of my other opinions as a young man, this one was rooted in ignorance.

Everything changed for me regarding my ideas about chiropractic care when I was 33 years old. While installing a power vent on my roof, I stood straight up quickly and wrenched my back. The common colloquialism is that I "threw out my back", but neither that phrase nor the word "wrenched" really seems to capture the pain and immobility I experienced. Those terms are woefully inadequate. I had to have a neighbor help me off the roof and for 15 days walked around (I use that term loosely) like Mel Brooks' *"Two Thousand Year Old Man"*.

It happened subsequently a couple of more times before I broke down and visited a chiropractor, wanting some relief other than a prognosis of taking a sharp blade to my spine. What I ultimately discovered was that I had a slight, possibly congenital, abnormality at the L4 position of my spine that could heretofore cause issues whenever I got out of alignment. Over the years, that diagnosis has played out as true and about once a year for the next twenty years or so (thankfully not more often than that) I had similar episodes, from picking up something awkwardly, or bending over wrong or twisting quickly in one direction. One time it went out when I just simply reached for an errant pass while playing basketball.

Now, in that previous paragraph, the essential word to focus on is "alignment". It's amazing how critically important that characteristic is to these marvelous spines God created and to the overall good health most of us enjoy. What I have found in my now monthly adjustments with my chiropractor is that even when I do not suffer some debilitating wrenching episode, in a month's time my spine gets out of alignment to the extent that one leg will be 1/8 to 1/4 inch longer (it's obviously not really longer but the unaligned tilt of my hips causes me to walk and stand as if that is physically the case).

Thankfully, it's been some time since that 1/8 to 1/4 inch misalignment has caused a major wrenching event, but more recently that drift out of alignment occasionally leaves me with a minor irritating pain in my back, hip or sometimes even down to my calf and ankle. Not painful enough to limit any activity but just painful enough to make it uncomfortable to sit for a long period of time or get to sleep without some pain medication.

Most of the time I don't even notice that I am out of alignment. I experience mild surprise when I have a pain free month and find I am still out of alignment. So now I am a chiropractic care **adherent**. I "religiously" have my spine readjusted to the standard that is appropriate for an aligned spine and I pay more careful attention between adjustments to my movements and activities so that I can enjoy good spinal health along with all the other things that accompany it. As you probably are aware, our spines are intricately interwoven with all of the functions of these bodies of ours that are *"fearfully and wonderfully made"* and good spinal health leads to the best chance that all other parts of our body will function optimally.

Now enough of my advertisement for the American Chiropractic Association. My goal here is to draw the analogy with our spiritual lives. For maturing Christians we must keep an eye on spiritual alignment as well, because it's just as easy to drift and get almost invisibly out of alignment with God's standard, to our spiritual detriment. In fact, the bible even warns us of our propensity to drift.

> *"Therefore we must pay much closer attention to what we have heard, lest we* ***drift away*** *from it." Hebrews 2:1*

That is why the bible mentions the topic of "obedience" over 300 times (not including the synonymous words and phrases in Psalms 119 and other similar passages). Obedience is the care we take to bring ourselves into alignment with God's commands, directives and designs for our lives - and to stay there - and for how we avoid self-inflicted spiritual wounds through disobedience. This is where we get the "A" for our acronym "FLAIR": **Adherence**. Obedience means we adhere to the teachings we have been learning as we have begun to follow Christ.

You may be wondering why I did not use "O" for obedience in my acronym (beside the fact that "FLOIR" doesn't spell anything and therefore would be a poor mnemonic device). It's not that obedience is an inadequate word, it's because "adherence" articulates some special qualities of obedience that I want to emphasize and have you remember. I am not suggesting "adherence" as a substitute for obedience, but rather as a megaphone to amplify important qualities about what is involved when we obey.

Of course, we have all been told since we were lads and lasses to "obey" our parents, our teachers, our bosses, to the point that the word, I am afraid, may have become watered down by our culture, especially a culture like today's that is so hostile to any type of authority. My sense is that "adherence" may offer the added emphasis to help recapture the importance of the term "obedience" for our culture and the generations to follow.

Said another way, when was the last time you were asked to "adhere" to something? Hopefully, in beckoning you that way, there is a freshness that is enticing and inviting. And well it should be, because the call to adherence is replete with great benefits.

ꟹ

Historically, the strong term "adherent" had a lot more usage in the past than it does today. Chalk it up to our culture's tendency to diminish the meaning and intensity of terms that once were important. This was brought home to me even as I was initially putting this teaching together. Back in the early 2000's when I first developed this FLAIR approach, there was a website called adherents.com that catalogued various statistics of religions all over the world. At the time, a striking statistic they reported indicated that in the world there were two billion adherents (their term) to Christianity, with 86% of Americans self-identifying that way. If you recall from a previous chapter, those statistics about the American part of that statement are definitely on the decline.

In fact, so is adherents.com, apparently. As I checked them out recently, I found that they can only be found as an archived website in the Library of Congress. They ended their run in 2019. Perhaps they got lazy with their domain registration, because if you Google their url today, you'll learn all about labs that study adhesives and glues. But more likely, people today don't seem to really adhere to much anymore. In fact, if you look at the dictionary definition of the medical application of the word "adherent", you find it is now a term that reveals how much a patient "*complies*" with a doctor's medical advice. Is it me, or does the word "*comply*" indicate a much weaker option to "*obey*"?

If you have attended church any length of time, you are well aware of the importance of obedience to the Christian faith, and it is a serious component of the action of adhering to those things that we have learned from Jesus. But I have adopted the term "adhere" for a reason, and not just because "obey" would have spoiled my FLAIR mnemonic, making it less memorable.

I want to suggest that there is a nuance to adhering that captures obeying and strengthens it, and I can make that point with a simple example, an object lesson that you can do for yourself to illustrate my point.

Allow me a sidebar for a moment. Sociologists claim that in the history of the earth there have been over 117 billion people who have lived. One might quibble with that number and question the methods sociologists have used to arrive at that estimation forensically, but we can say with certainty that almost 8 billion of them are alive today as we speak. Most dwell in anonymity and never experience any fame, just living out their lives and rarely affecting the lives of their fellow men on anything resembling a global scale. But, every now and then we read of someone who, though fairly anonymous, makes a monumental impact on the culture.

In that vein, most readers will not recognize the name Vesta Stoudt. Vesta was the mother of two young sons who both served in the Navy during World War II. Her war effort was to work in a factory packing and inspecting ammunition boxes. At that time, those boxes were sealed with a paper tape, and the entire box dipped in wax to make it waterproof. The boxes were hard to open and the opening tab on the tape often broke, so Vesta had an idea to create a waterproof, cloth based tape that could be used to seal boxes of ammunition so that they could be easily accessed by soldiers reloading under fire. Originally, her employer did not see the profit value in this, so she wrote to President Franklin D. Roosevelt with this idea. He was so taken with it that he ordered it created. A company named Johnson & Johnson created it. Maybe you have heard of them...they *have* made a recognized impact on society. The product that was born was so easy to open it was originally called the "*100 mile an hour tape*". Today it has a simpler name and it can be found in almost every household: duct tape!

Perhaps you have begun to wonder why I have launched into this parenthetic about the history of duct tape, but bear with me, I have a point to make and I would like you to further indulge me in a small experiment that I think will greatly illuminate the topic of this chapter.

Go out to your garage or check out your junk drawer and take out a roll of duct tape. Now tear off a piece and stick it to something. Anything. Now carefully remove it. Depending on what you applied it to and what that material's surface tension is, it may be easy or a little more difficult to remove.

Now step two: tear off two pieces of duct tape and stick them together, adhesive face to adhesive face. Now take them apart.

I'll wait....

Still waiting.

What you undoubtedly have discovered is that it is nearly impossible to separate them. That is the power of adherence. And, that is the example of the type of adherence Christ wants in our lives. Our obedience is often represented by the first example where we stick to what we have been taught. But none of those things that we applied it to in the first example had any adherent quality of their own and so we often find ourselves pulling away from what we initially obeyed, similar to how you were able to pull the tape off whatever you applied it to.

But with Christ, His part is already "sticky"! He has demonstrated that for us in Matthew 28: 19-20:

> *"Therefore go and make disciples of all nations, baptizing them in the name of the Father and of the Son and of the Holy Spirit, and teaching them to obey everything I have commanded you. And surely* ***I am with you always,*** *to the very end of the age."*

As maturing disciples, Jesus, who is sticking with us, beckons us to "stick" to His teachings as our part of the adhering process. Obedience is a critical part and will be the majority of what this chapter discusses, but obedience is strengthened by the fact that Jesus is always with us. In fact, Jesus also explains it using another "a" word: *abiding*. See John 15:4:

> *"Abide in me, and I in you. As the branch cannot bear fruit by itself, unless it abides in the vine, neither can you, unless you abide in me."*

As I mentioned in the previous chapters, these five areas of discipleship determine how we can develop into the mature disciples God intends us to become. As a reminder, these five areas are:

- Following Jesus (and all that entails)
- Learning from Jesus
- Adhering to what He teaches us
- Imitating Jesus (conforming to His image)
- Replicating this growth in other disciples on that same narrow path

To remember this (and also the chronology involved which I believe is of utmost importance), I am reminding you again that I am using the acronym **FLAIR** (the first letters of each of the above five areas) and this chapter will be on the third element: *adhering to what we learn from Jesus*.

Like many of the most instructive passages in the New Testament, Jesus, and later the writers of the epistles, followed a common pattern in teaching how we are to live. An example of this pattern, for instance, can be found studying what has been called *"the Ladder of Virtues"* in 2nd Peter 1:5-9.

> *"5For this very reason, make every effort to add to your faith goodness; and to goodness, knowledge; 6and to knowledge, self-control; and to self-control, perseverance; and to perseverance, godliness; 7and to godliness, mutual affection; and to mutual affection, love. 8For if you possess these qualities in increasing measure, they will keep you from being ineffective and unproductive in your knowledge of our Lord Jesus Christ. 9But whoever does not have them is nearsighted and blind, forgetting that they have been cleansed from their past sins".*

Instructions in these passages typically start off with teaching on transformation on the inside and then move to transformation on the outside that is visible to others. Adherence is the step where we begin to really see that transformation in these five elements of a maturing disciple.

Following and learning begin primarily as internal issues of commitment. Adherence is where our growth in discipleship is cemented in that internal commitment but begins to manifest itself more visibly to the external. Take a look in the Old Testament at 2nd Kings 17:34:

> *"To this day they persist in their former practices. They neither worship the LORD nor adhere to the decrees and ordinances, the laws and commands that the LORD gave the descendants of Jacob, whom he named Israel."*

Even in the Old Testament, adherence to the Word of God was a **visibly expressive example** set alongside our public worship as the two ways others could determine whether we were followers of God or not.

A Working Definition

How do we transport this term from the Old Testament to our modern day lives and maintain this expression of visible obedience? The word "*adhere*" is not a word, in our modern vernacular, that we often associate any longer with followers or disciples. It is related to a Latin root word for "*adhesive, adhesion*", and that is the more common usage for the word today.

Nonetheless, historically it has provided a more than adequate descriptive term for the type of disciples we ought to be and it would behoove us to come up with a good working definition going forward. Consider the three primary definitions we see of this word in the English dictionary. The first dictionary definition should come as no surprise:

- *"to stick fast or together by (or as if by) grasping, suction or being glued"*. In botany, plants that grow together or are fused together are called adherents. Consider the "branch" and the "vine" metaphor in John 15 as a scriptural teaching that reflects this botanical definition.

The second definition or usage is as follows:

- *"to be devoted as a follower or supporter"*

And finally, the last of the three major meanings of this word:

- *"to follow closely, to carry out without deviation"*

Combining the three definition points, we come up with a very good working theology on what it means to be an adherent to Christ:

A devoted follower who 'sticks fast' to Christ's teachings without deviation.

Given this definition, how many of us can claim that title of adherent? If you are like me, perhaps the "without deviation" part can sometimes be the stumbling block because it sounds out of the realm of possibility. But be reminded of the constant commands we have from our Lord in the Bible to be holy, pure, perfect, blameless... all words that may sound like they are setting an unreachable standard, but nonetheless connote an unwavering commitment to follow what Jesus commanded and taught.

ᘓ

What Reigns in You?

The Apostle Paul echoes this type of commitment in his writings. Beginning in Romans 6:12, he takes us through a process of giving up our desires, becoming slaves to righteousness and ending up with holiness (verse 22).

First, Paul declares that we obey that which reigns in us (Romans 6:12). If Christ reigns in us, we obey Him. If sin reigns in us, we obey the flesh. Examine yourself.... who is reigning in you? John Donne, an English theologian in the 17th century said *"to adhere to an enemy is to become an enemy"*. Likewise, if we are more stuck on our fleshly inclinations, then we become like the world. But when we adhere to Christ, we become like Him.

Secondly, that which we obey, we become slaves of, and becoming a slave means we also receive all the consequences of being a slave. If we are slaves to sin, the consequence is death (this is the state of the unbeliever). However, if we are slaves to obedience we benefit with righteousness ("righteousness" comes to us from the old English "right-wiseness", reminding us that righteousness describes a state of being right with God).

Form

Next, the vehicle for reaching this way of adherence is the "form of teaching" with which we have been entrusted. Let's focus on these two important points: "*entrusting*" and "*form*". Being entrusted reinforces the responsibility we talked about in the last chapter with regard to the responsibility that arises from our endeavor at learning ("*bringing out the treasures*" as a directive to share what we have learned).

The "form" of teaching is the gospel, the Word. Here the word "form" is the Greek *typos* ("pattern, example, model"). The metaphor that comes to mind here is of a mold which is formed, into which molten material is poured. The gospel is the mold and we are the material poured into that mold. If we conform ourselves to the mold by obeying the teaching then we come out looking like what the gospel tells us about (Jesus Christ).

When I was in college, I worked at my church which was near downtown Houston. We had a recreation building that had a gym, game room and upstairs classrooms. One of those classrooms was used to teach ceramics classes to immigrants who were living close to the church. The church had two kilns and about one hundred two-piece ceramic molds.

One of my jobs was to take bags of clay slip, a kind of clay slurry, and pour them into the molds and then wrap large rubber bands around the molds to hold them together securely while they dried. Sounds pretty simple, but the early results showed me there was more involved in getting the final product just right. A lot of my vases certainly did not look like vases. You had to get just the right mix of water and clay, had to use the correct strength bands to keep the molds from separating and leaking before they dried, and most importantly, you had to know just how long to leave everything in the mold. Too short and the finished piece wouldn't hold its shape, too long and it was too brittle and hard to remove cleanly from the mold.

After a while, I got very good at this and was able to produce hundreds of perfect little figurines, vases and knick-knacks ready for painting and firing. All that said, I hope it is obvious that I am drawing a parallel with the mold of the Scripture which requires in the same way that we spend time learning all the ways the text leads us and guides us so that we look like what we are intended to be.

In addition, I hope I have not understated the quality of the clay slip that was poured into the molds. The success of the finished product, which was dependent on proper timing and securing banding of the two halves of the molds together, also depended on the proper *consistency* of the ingredients of the clay to the water. Likewise, *consistency* in our obedience is just as important an element because it results in our properly obeying those tenets we have learned from the Word.

Continuing with Paul's process in Romans 6, we observe his fourth point begins with one of the greatest self-examination questions in scripture in verse 21:

> *"What benefit did you reap at that time from the things you are now ashamed of?"*

What a great question to examine the past as well as guard against future issues. We can and should look at any possible action or decision with these questions on our lips: *"How will that benefit me?"* or *"will I be ashamed of that?"*

Lastly, our obedience leads to holiness (Romans 6:22) and the result is eternal life. When we ask ourselves *"how can one be holy as the Scripture exhorts?"* we must answer that we can only become holy by taking the path of obedience. The first rung of that ladder is to obediently receive Christ as your Savior. The result of eternal life, which begins at that moment of salvation, is the journey of pouring our lives into the mold of the gospel.

Let's see how close this lines up with Jesus' own description. But before we do, let's answer the question that may be brewing with regard to whether this was a characteristic that was indeed a part of what Jesus sought in His disciples and whether they accomplished it.

In Matthew 12:47-50 we read,

> [47] *"Someone told him, "Your mother and brothers are standing outside, wanting to speak to you."* [48] *He replied to him, "Who is my mother, and who are my brothers?"* [49] *Pointing to his disciples, he said, "Here are my mother and my brothers.* [50] *For whoever **does the will***

*of **my Father** in heaven is my brother and sister and mother".*

Jesus used the phrase *"doing God's will"* to describe the process and discipline of adhering. As you can see, the visibility of our discipleship nature is not the only thing that undergoes change as we begin to adhere to what we have learned. The determinant of which "will" we commit to follow changes as well.

When we follow Jesus and begin to actively proceed to learn from Him, we begin to see that part of our maturation involves undergoing a change from what *we* desire to what *Jesus* desires. That is truly transformation, and it sets us apart (this setting apart is the very definition of sanctification) from the world. Here's why:

The will of God involves a change from my desires (world's) to God's. We see that in the parable of the hidden treasure when we look at Matthew 13:44. In that parable, the man who found the treasure (God's will for his life) was willing to forsake everything he valued to have it. That was a huge change. We see it also in 1 John 2:17:

"The world and its desires pass away, but the man who does the will of God lives forever."

And in 1 Peter 4:2:

"As a result, he does not live the rest of his earthly life for evil

human desires, but rather for the will of God."

Jesus made a great exchange, His blood for our sins. And, now we must make one as well in the form of surrender, our will for His. Jesus uses what I call the first of three "marks of the disciple" (things that "brand" us as His devoted followers) to describe this principle. In John 8:21 we read:

"To the Jews who had believed him, Jesus said, "If you hold to my teaching, you are really my disciples."

Here the word "*hold*" (the Greek word is *meno*) really means more than grasping, but instead means "abiding", allowing His teachings to "live" in us. The noun form of the word from which "*hold*" is translated is seen in John 14:2 where it is translated as "*rooms*". Rooms give a building form, function, structure, purpose and order. In the same way the teachings of Jesus provide those identical attributes for our lives.

Evidence

In John 14, Jesus beseeched the Jews to view the evidence of His miracles as proof that the Father was in Him. He could have required signs and miracles of us to prove we are His followers, a requirement that would go largely unfulfilled in most lives. Instead, He simply beckons us to live a life that is wrapped up in adhering to His teachings. In other words, let his teachings give our lives form, function, structure, purpose and order.

The first mark of a disciple, then, is obedience. This is synonymous with the idea of adhering to what we have learned from Jesus. I give the best evidence of being in God's will when I adhere to and obey what Jesus taught. (Marks number two and number three, by the way, are visible as well: loving one another and bearing spiritual fruit).

Principles of Adherence

Let me close this chapter with these principles of adherence that come to us from a careful examination of God's Word. Combining them with the affirmation of Christ's remaining in us produces that adherence that is so essential in our quest for maturity of our faith.

Obedience amplifies our ability to hear God. The Greek word for obedience (*hupakoe*) means literally to "hear under" (the second part of that Greek word, *akoe*, is where we get our English word "acoustics"). If you have ever been to the Texas state capital (or any other domed building) and stood in the center under the dome, you have experienced the excellent acoustics when you are perfectly located right under the apex.

Obedience is how we join God in His work. Henry Blackaby pointed out in his seminal work *Experiencing God* that we all experience the following at some point:

- Crisis of faith. This leads to faith and action

- Action leads to an adjustment (change) we must make
- Adjustment is our preparation for obedience

Obedience reveals what we really believe about God.

- Obedience in the little things leads to bigger tasks and opportunities because we know God wants us on mission with Him
- Obedience is the best way to determine the pattern of how God works in our lives. See John 12:26

"Whoever serves me must follow me; and where I am, my servant also will be. My Father will honor the one who serves me."

Obedience is the manner in which we come to know God's will. See Romans 12:1-2.

"[1] Therefore, I urge you, brothers and sisters, in view of God's mercy, to offer your bodies as a living sacrifice, holy and pleasing to God—this is your true and proper worship. [2] Do not conform to the pattern of this world, but be transformed by the renewing of your mind. Then you will be able to test and approve what God's will is—his good, pleasing and perfect will."

Obedience determines whether we will grow in intimacy with God. King David's great 51st Psalm is a breathtaking example of his vulnerability, transparency and understanding. Note verse 6:

"Behold, you delight in truth in the inward being, and you teach me

wisdom in the secret heart."

When we think about it, God's wisdom and truth in my inward being and my secret heart is a perfect definition of the spiritual intimacy we seek with our Creator.

Obedience is the entry point to learning how to imitate our Lord. This leads us into the fourth area of discipleship growth in the following chapter.

Questions for Discussion

The progression from inward commitments to outward expression is one that is an essential part of our growth curve. What part of this is most noticeable in the people around you?

How does the idea of adherence strengthen your attitude toward obedience?

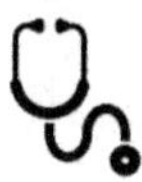

Picking up on Paul's teachings in Romans 6, what reigns in you?

Chapter Nine

"You were made unique...do not die a copy."

–Norman Barnes

Imitating Jesus

In 1897, Charles Sheldon published his Christian classic *In His Steps*. It has sold more that 50 million copies which even today, where we see an explosion of book publishing, is astounding. It's all the more remarkable because of when it was published and how difficult it was to get the books to the masses in that era. No Amazon, no Kindle, no Christianbook.com, no Lifeway. But, nonetheless, at one time in the early twentieth century, his book was the most widely published book in the world not called "The Bible".

It began as a series of sermons that Sheldon delivered over a year to his congregation and which were ultimately novelized as a story of a small church that committed to spend a year doing nothing without first asking the question, "*What would Jesus do?*".

Perhaps that question sounds familiar, and it should. In the 1990's a movement, complete with a WWJD bracelet, took the Christian culture by storm, compelling a new generation of believers to seek to imitate Jesus in ever decision and action, filtering everything they did through that same question.

The world tells us that "imitation is the sincerest form of flattery". As usual, the world has a pitifully tepid view of those attributes that God finds desirable and necessary to propel Christian disciples toward their potential as kingdom difference-makers.

In this chapter, we'll look at the complete blossoming of the visible aspect of our walk. Whereas adhering to Jesus' teachings was both internal (where obedience always begins) as well as the beginning of an external manifestation of His commands, imitation takes us all the way to a place where our motivation is not just to improve our walk, but indeed it is to demonstrate our walk. So, imitate is the "I" in the acronym FLAIR.

More than fifty years ago I began my college career in the architecture program at the University of Houston and in first year design classes we were taught "*form follows function*". That was stressed partly because architecture students typically get too caught up in building "pretty" things that don't work, rather than first focusing on the function and letting that lead to the form. It also happens to be a truism that spans many aspects of our lives including our spiritual walk.

In the last chapter we discussed how obedience (adhering or holding to Jesus' teaching) was akin to the thing that gave structure, function and purpose to our lives much like rooms give the same to the shell of a building (recall that the word "hold" in its noun form is also translated "rooms" in John 14:2). In this chapter, we will now talk about the "form" that follows our "function".

If we ask the question: "*What is my function?*" then we should answer "to do God's will" or "to glorify God". Indeed, in the very first answer in the Westminster shorter catechism which Christians have been affirming for nearly 400 years, we respond to the question "*what is the chief end of man*" with the answer "*to glorify God and enjoy Him forever*". We best enjoy God when we are in harmony with His will.

We have seen that our adherence to Jesus' teachings is instrumental to our ability to function the way God intends. However, now there follows a second question beyond what function we should have: "*What shall I look like when I am carrying out my function?*". This is the form that follows the function.

Often, we get so focused on sharing doctrinal points concerning the death of Jesus that we forget how much there is to expound upon about the life of Jesus. In 1 Peter 2:21 Peter relates to us the biblical "*in His steps*":

> *"For to this you have been called, because Christ also suffered for you, leaving you an example, so that you might follow in his steps."*

Jesus' life is displayed in exquisite detail in the Word so that we might observe the example that we should follow, and do so in a manner visible to others. Specifically, Peter addresses a calling to suffer, by following Jesus' example and following in His steps. But suffering is not the only way we follow in His steps. The entirety of that chapter gives examples of how we are to shed our fleshly characteristics and adopt Jesus' characteristics in our life instead.

In his classic *Celebration of Discipline*, Richard Foster calls this following of Jesus' example "*imitatio Christi*" or "*imitatio divina*". Foster explains this in English this way: "*His living provides us a paradigm for our living*". Foster goes on to define Jesus' prayer tradition, His holiness, His Spirit-empowered ministry and other aspects of His life as examples of how His living was designed to give us a pattern for our living as mature disciples.

Jesus Himself, within the framework of Teacher with His students, exhorts us to this end in Matthew 10:24-25.

> 24 *"A student is not above his teacher, nor a servant above his master.*
> 25 *It is enough for the student to be like his teacher, and the servant like his master."*

These words to His students contrast with the fundamental belief of the New Age, that we would ourselves become gods, which is a heretical belief at its core. Jesus tells us essentially that we aren't to be divine, but rather imitate His divine characteristics and qualities.

ꟹ

Let me interject here that one of the main problems with Christians today is that many are *impersonating* Jesus instead of *imitating* Him. What is the difference? Imitating means "*to model oneself after the behavior or actions of another; to copy their appearance, mannerisms and/or speech*".

Impersonating, on the other hand, means *"to act the part"*. Impersonating is, by nature, a charade. We've all played the game "Charades" before. We employ clues such as "*sounds like*". In other words, it is not really that but it "*sounds like it*". And when that clue doesn't work, we are left to offer one that can tend to be even more obscure, in order to get the Charades participants to guess at the right answer. This begs an important question: how often does the way we live out our faith make the gospel more obscure rather than make it clearer? Do we really want others to have to "*guess*" at the substance of our lives in Christ or, rather, for it to appear abundantly evident?

A fundamental truth about imitation is this: **You can only accurately imitate one thing**. So, imitating Jesus will, by definition, prevent us from imitating the world, which will automatically make us beneficial to the kingdom. Of course, a quick look around the Church will convince us that not every member of the

Body of Christ has tapped into this powerful truth, as we see many who present a very blurred view of Christ. Like the "Charades" player, they are often *pretending* at things that are of utmost importance to the life of a disciple. Hopefully, this observation amplifies the point of the previous chapters, that without fully understanding how to follow Jesus, learn from Him, and adhere to His teachings and commands, we can not hope to accurately display Him to a lost and fallen world.

We see this principle of resembling that which we imitate at work in 2 Kings 17:1:

> *"They rejected his decrees and the covenant he had made with their fathers and the warnings he had given them. They followed worthless idols and themselves became worthless. They imitated the nations around them although the LORD had ordered them, "Do not do as they do," and they did the things the LORD had forbidden them to do."*

The quickest way to become worthless in kingdom work is to imitate something other than Christ. And while imitating Christ may seem an awesome, insurmountable task, when we search through the text for specifics, we indeed find a large number of things Jesus did that we could and should emulate. When we make this search and observe our Lord, we find we can break down the imitation part of our discipleship journey into three general categories: "Counting the cost", "Focusing on the recipients of our ministry", and "Covering everything with agape love". Let's look at each one individually.

ఽ

Category #1: Counting the Cost

Often we are most challenged by passages about Jesus' life that have the sparsest details. This may be because when we don't have as much information as we think we need to form an opinion or make a decision, we often resort to heuristic thinking. Heuristic thinking is our way of making mental shortcuts (often with inordinate use of assumptions) to help us fill in the blanks so that we can proceed toward a decision or action. The passage describing the forty days Jesus spent in the wilderness is undoubtedly one such passage. Matthew devotes only eleven verses to these forty days and the dramatic things that occurred there which Jesus used to launch His public ministry. Though Matthew's focus is on the battle between Jesus and the tempter, there is undoubtedly much more that occurred in the way of Jesus counting the cost of the three years of ministry that lay before Him. That cost-counting had three elements, which lead to us asking three important questions of ourselves.

PRICE : *What price are we willing to pay?* In Luke 14, Jesus reminds us there are at least three main things we must be willing to sacrifice if we desire to pursue discipleship. In verse 26, we read this:

> *"If anyone comes to me and does not hate his father and mother, his wife and children, his brothers and sisters —yes, even his own life*

—he cannot be my disciple".

Jesus is not commanding hate here. That word is used simply as a contrast in devotion. Our devotion to Christ must be so great that all other loyalties pale in comparison. He continues in verse 27:

"And anyone who does not carry his cross and follow me cannot be my disciple".

Much has been made throughout the last 2,000 years as to what our "*cross carrying*" must look like. In January of 2025 Andrew Blessitt, a Christian evangelist, passed away at the age of 84. Blessitt was best known for carrying a twelve foot, one hundred ten pound cross for over fifty years all over the world as part of his evangelistic ministry. His walking journeys, carrying his cross, covered almost 45,000 miles, earning him the Guinness Book of World Records distinction for the Longest Walk. More importantly, it offered him a multitude of opportunities to share the gospel of Jesus Christ to tens of thousands of people.

It should go without saying that each of us may manifest this in a different way, but, essentially, Jesus is warning us that there will be the need to sacrifice something which will take us out of our comfort zone. Finally, in Luke 14, verse 33:

"In the same way, those of you who do not give up everything you have cannot be my disciples."

Historically, the ascetics (from a Greek word meaning "hermit") turned this verse into their literal theology by "offloading" every material thing and living the simplest life possible. Here, as with the families spoken about in Luke 14, Jesus is warning that the price of discipleship means things we treasure aren't necessarily evil or meant to be avoided because many of them are blessings from God. However, they must take second place to the call of the kingdom. And if they don't, they must be removed and dispensed with.

PLANS: The second question is *What should characterize our plans?* The word "completion" comes to mind first. We see this in Jesus' self-description in John 17:4.

> *"I glorified you on earth, having* ***accomplished*** *the work that you gave me to do."*

"Effectiveness" would be a second characteristic that Jesus illustrates in His planning for us to emulate. Both of these combine to establish our fruitfulness (see John 16). When we say "*Jesus is good*", it means He is effective (the word "good" in the bible comes from a word that at its root means "*it works*"). Our planning should reflect the goal of being effective and fruitful when that work pursues its completeness.

STEADFASTNESS: And, finally our third self-directed question: *What will be a non-negotiable?* Compromise has become second nature in our culture. It permeates our political system, the business world and often our churches. At the end of the forty days, the devil tempted Jesus, and He showed us three areas that were, for Him, non-negotiables (see Matthew 4:3-10).

- The Word of God was a non-negotiable for Jesus.
- Trusting in God's plan was a second non-negotiable.
- Thirdly, full devotion to the Lord God only was a final non-negotiable.

Each of these are to be absolute non-negotiables for us as well.

Looking again at the passage in Luke 14 in verse 34, Jesus continues with a subject that suggests another non-negotiable area for us: our character:

> *"Salt is good, but if it loses its saltiness, how can it be made salty again? It is fit neither for the soil nor for the manure pile; it is thrown out. He who has ears to hear, let him hear."*

To understand the significance of Jesus' analogy, consider the attributes of salt that were appreciated in biblical times:

- In that culture it had great value.
- Salt was unstained and thus represented purity.
- Salt provided flavor.
- Salt had important preserving qualities.
- Salt would sting when rubbed in a wound, acting often as

a necessary irritant, calling attention to the danger of infection.
- Salt created thirst.
- Salt was associated with cleanliness, as we see in the practice of shepherds rubbing new-born lambs with salt as a way of cleaning them from their afterbirth.

The saltiness of our character should be the part we mark "non-negotiable". Paul says it this way in Colossians 4:6:

> *"Let your conversation be always full of grace, seasoned with salt, so that you may know how to answer everyone".*

Each of those qualities about actual salt has a corresponding spiritual connotation in our character. Consider what we express in our character when we match up the way we live with salt's valuable characteristics:

- *Value:* In a culture that has fallen on the rocks, our character can act as a beacon for others to follow.
- *Purity:* Our character should define purity in a culture that has grown anything but pure.
- *Flavor:* The Greek word for "saint" (*haggios*) has as its root meaning "different". When our character is different from what is normally seen in the world, we become noticeable just as the flavor in a food is most noticeable.
- *Preservation:* Maintaining a Christian character helps preserve those things that were once rightly the norm instead

of the exception.

- *Irritant:* Sometimes the words we speak out of our character may need to be direct and actually sting a bit in order for someone we are ministering to or discipling better see danger that lies ahead or become aware of a blind spot in their behavior.
- *Thirst:* Our Jesus-imitating character should create a desire in others to emulate that which satisfies our deepest needs.
- *Cleanliness:* Our character and the life that emanates from it will help others clean up the mess of their own lives as they seek to model their lives after Christ as well.

❧

Category #2: Focus

As we embark on category number two, let me address something that is a little bit obvious. Hopefully you have noticed, by now, that I have sprinkled Greek words in this and previous chapters as a way of better illuminating meanings intended in the original manuscripts that can lead to questions when translated into English. Historically, bible students have stepped outside of their native tongues and investigated the Hebrew and Greek languages in an attempt to better understand what was originally written. Scholars refer to this as "going back to the fountain" as a way of gleaning original meaning from the text. This chapter on *Imitating* probably has more of that than other chapters. Hopefully, it is not overwhelming but rather intended to put a thought in your mind that there are good tools which are available to all disciples that can open up insights into the Word if you make use of them. Let me mention three such tools that I would recommend in any student's library, that have been most beneficial to someone like me who is *not* a Greek or Hebrew scholar.

- **An exhaustive concordance** Most bibles have a partial concordance in the back, but an exhaustive one will have every word in the text along with its Greek or Hebrew version. When you get an exhaustive concordance, make sure it is one that matches the translation of the bible that you most frequently study. That will make it much easier to get maximum benefit out of its use.
- **Vines Expository Commentary on New Testament Words.** One of my favorites, this book has definitions and usages of each Greek word found in the New Testament and will be very helpful for the disciple who is focusing his or her study on the New Covenant doctrine.
- **IVP Bible Dictionary**. This bypasses translation from Greek or Hebrew to English, but like a regular dictionary provides important definitions of words found in the text.

Those are three of a multitude of helpful study aids that are available no matter what level of student you are or desire to become.

Now back to the category of *Focus*. Focusing on the recipients of our ministry is the second category in which we show ourselves to be like Christ. Spend a moment reading Luke 4:16-21, and let's note two things: first, the spiritual connotations in Jesus' words, and second, the parallel between Jesus' self description and the description of born-again believing disciples, members of His Body, His Church.

"[16] He went to Nazareth, where he had been brought up, and on the Sabbath day he went into the synagogue, as was his custom. He stood up to read, [17] and the scroll of the prophet Isaiah was handed to him. Unrolling it, he found the place where it is written: [18] "The Spirit of the Lord is on me, because he has anointed me to proclaim good news to the poor. He has sent me to proclaim freedom for the prisoners and recovery of sight for the blind to set the oppressed free, [19] to proclaim the year of the Lord's favor." [20] Then he rolled up the scroll, gave it back to the attendant and sat down. The eyes of everyone in the synagogue were fastened on him. [21] He began by saying to them, "Today this scripture is fulfilled in your hearing."

Isaiah's words, which are recorded in this passage in Luke, lay out the message Jesus now wants His followers to observe in His life and to emulate in their own. If we approach this with an eye toward the careful grammar of the passage, we see each statement in the passage largely breaks down into a verb, its direct object (the noun which receives the action or effect of the verb) and the corresponding indirect objects (those who receive the action of the direct object). Clarity comes as we explore each of these grammatic elements and their relative significance. The Greek will also assist us with this clarity.

Central to this passage's message is the repetition of the word "proclaim" which in this passage is the verb. It is used three times and implied once more in the compound statement of proclaiming both freedom and recovery of sight. It is the Greek word *kerusso* and is often translated interchangeably with "preach". Its synonyms are "heralding" and "publishing" in other passages (see Mark 1:45, for example), the latter giving it a flavor of "*spreading*" the news, whereas the preaching of the gospel above denotes the action and duty to *relate* the cheerful news.

Isn't there something immediately evident by the repetition of the action of proclamation? Despite the many things Jesus exhorts His church to do (and there are many other great things we are called to), proclamation of the good news must be the hub from which all other things extend. In other words, any work we do as individuals or, as a church, that does not have at its core the spreading of the gospel to the lost and the message of our joy at growing in our faith to other disciples, needs to be revisited.

Moving onto the direct objects (those subjects that are to be related, heralded, spread, and taught), we see four different things Jesus Himself focuses on and by extension, we are to focus on. It is by no means an exhaustive list for us, but one wherein we should be sure we always cover. Here are the four direct objects with their corresponding indirect objects:

good news	poor
freedom	prisoners
recovery of sight	blind
year of the Lord's favor	all (in Luke, to the Jews present)

THE POOR: Looking at the direct and indirect objects in tandem, we can see what Jesus is driving at. In "*proclaiming the good news to the poor*", Jesus is directing us to preach the gospel directed at those He calls the poor, not necessarily who we would consider in that group.

But what is meant by poor? The Greek for poor here (*ptochos*) describes the nature of the person as one "*totally dependent on someone else and devoid of their own resources*", as opposed to a more economics-related statement of someone's financial condition (which would be *penichros* as in Luke 21:2). Jesus is describing the same folks He spoke of on the Sermon on the Mount:

"Blessed are the poor in spirit, for theirs is the kingdom of heaven."

Our duty as Jesus followers is to herald a message of joy and good news to those who find themselves totally dependent on the grace of God and His infinite mercy to bring salvation and the Kingdom into their lives. This would be to all, those who John described in John 3:16 as the "world".

PRISONERS AND THE OPPRESSED: The Greek word *apostello* is used here and translated as "sent", a familiar word which we see today as "*apostle*". This word represents an official and authoritative sending, an expression denoting the mission to be fulfilled and the authority to back it up. We have been sent by Jesus with the mission and authority to do what Jesus next mentions in the Luke 4 passage:

"...to proclaim freedom for the prisoners...".

"Freedom" is translated from *aphesis* which in virtually every other case is translated "forgiveness". It means dismissal or release and in the Septuagint (the Greek translation of the Old Testament) it is only associated with the Year of Jubilee.

In all other references in the Old Testament, the word *paresis* is used which means a covering in the remission of sin. Thus, the covenant of the law only covered sins, whereas the covenant Jesus brought would dismiss them.

Finally, who are the prisoners? The Greek describes them as *aichmalotos* or literally those taken by the spear (captives). They are prisoners of war in the spiritual battle between God and Satan. The spear, being a weapon of warfare, points to the spiritual battle that wages over men and results in many being captive to sin.

Now, skip down one:

"...to release the oppressed..."

This seemingly has a similar meaning. "Release" is also translated from *aphesis* meaning to liberate by way of forgiveness. However, the target audience here is the "oppressed" or literally those bruised and broken by calamity (*thrauo*). While the Jew could easily identify with those beaten into submission and taken prisoner, Jesus would have us reflect on who are the real imprisoned and oppressed, the common denominators being forgiveness and liberation. The targets become those who are spiritually afflicted (captives to sin) as well as those who have been physically and emotionally beaten by the chaos of this world system.

Christ would have us reach out equally to these, for just as the source of their calamity is identical both spiritually and physically, so is the Source of their liberation for both. Later in His ministry, Jesus emphasized this point when He gave special attention to the physical needs:

> *"For I was hungry and you gave me something to eat, I was thirsty and you gave me something to drink, I was a stranger and you invited me in, I needed clothes and you clothed me, I was sick and you looked after me, I was in prison and you came to visit me."* Matthew 25:36-44.

THE BLIND: Now, back to the previous one that was skipped:

> *"...recovery of sight for the blind..."*

This phrase is translated from *anablepsis* and means literally "to see again" or "to look up". It is used to indicate receiving or recovering sight. Interestingly, it is always used with the physical condition of blindness. Looking at the circumstances and the results of the receiving of sight, we see how Jesus and the apostles used this physical situation as a living metaphor for spiritual blindness. Note the progression we see through the Gospels with the same incident and finally through Paul's own experience of recovering sight that adds the final emphasis.

Matthew 20:34: Upon receiving sight the men followed Jesus
Mark 10:52: They received their sight **by faith** and followed Jesus
Luke 18:43: Received sight by faith, followed Jesus, and **praised God**
Acts 9:17: Saw again by faith, followed Jesus, praised God and **received the Holy Spirit**

TO ALL: Going back to the Luke 3 passage, if the term "recovery" is a sticking point (as in "*How can we recover that which we never had, namely spiritual sight?*"), consider three definitions for recovery which fit very nicely with the condition of our spiritual sight:

- the return to a normal condition (i.e., the condition God intended as normal)
- obtaining something usable from something unusable (e.g., silver recovery from exposed film)
- a favorable judgment in a legal verdict (a benefit)

This idea of recovery extends itself into the idea of restoration which is the immediate subject the Jews in attendance would have been focused on. It hearkens back to the Old Testament teaching of the Year of Jubilee when all prisoners and slaves were released and all debts forgiven. It is no wonder that in Luke's passage in chapter 4, the immediate reaction from the Jews (ironically, it depicts a perfect example for us as imitators) was that their eyes were **fastened** on Him. The Greek word *atenizo* which comes from a root that means "strain", finds its clearest meaning in the English words derived from it: "tense", "intensity", "attention". We cannot imitate Jesus unless we give Him our full attention, an attention that enables us to proclaim the promises of being restored, effective and beneficial to His kingdom plans.

❧

Category #3: Covering Everything With Agape Love

Covering everything with love is what Jesus called the second mark of the disciple, the mark being the visible way people will recognize who you are and Who you follow. All three of these marks are in the gospel of John, while all the essential actions associated with them are in the book of Matthew. It's as if God, in His wisdom, gave us one perspective that focused on what we should become and one that focused on how others will recognize it.

Regarding the mark of love, in John 13:34 we read:

> *"A new command I give you: Love one another. As I have loved you, so you must love one another. By this all men will know that*

you are my disciples, if you love one another."

This statement followed on the "heels" of (no pun intended) Jesus' foot-washing example where He renounced, among other things, reciprocal behavior in service. Again, Jesus' overriding concern was that these disciples project a clear message to the world of who they followed by this second mark: **how they loved one another.** This love is the agape style love which is unconditional, unmerited, action oriented, God-type love that seeks the highest benefit for the other. One of my favorite definitions of agape love is given to us by the scholar William Barclay: "*unconquerable benevolence*".

The standard of this conduct was the way Jesus has loved us. Clearly, it is a call for us to imitate Him. The beautiful thing about this example of love is that it has 3 benefits:

- It provides a model for how we are to behave
- It shows the world the primary characteristic of His nature (even the world knows that adherents and devotees resemble their master)
- It provides an appealing feature to draw men to Christ. People want to be the recipients of love.

Counting the cost of ministry...focusing on the recipients of that ministry...covering it all with Christ-like love. These are the primary ways we, as disciples, represent our Master visibly and are well-conformed to His image. In this way, we are both fruitful in our behavior and good works and, at the same time, best represent who Jesus is to those who do not yet know Him or to those who do but are yearning for a greater understanding of His nature and character.

-Questions for Discussion

Which of the three categories represented a new way of looking at ways we can imitate Jesus?

What are the ways that agape love is different from every other type of love expressed in your life?

In what ways do you see that Christ's life is providing a new paradigm for your life?

Chapter Ten

"We cannot direct the wind,

but we can adjust the sails."

–Dolly Parton

Replicating Yourself

The previous chapter was a discussion on the pattern, or example, Christ left us so that as we mature as disciples, we know how to show the world Who we follow, Who we learn from, Whose teachings we adhere to and Who we imitate. Finally, we reach the last of the five primary elements of our sanctification, which is summed up in one question: *how do we help others experience the same growth we have experienced?* Or, to put it in the context of our Great Commission, *how do we make disciples?*

To see the end game, in Jesus' mind, let's take a look at our marvelous bodies. In every one of the thirty trillion (or so), cells in our body there is a template found in the nucleus of that cell, referred to as our DNA. This complex two-stranded molecule is responsible for replicating itself trillions of times in order to form new identical cells, 40-60 times for each cell in that cell's life cycle. Each day this process results in over 300 billion new cells replacing old ones.

Those new cells are needed for us to grow from an ovum to a baby, to grow from a baby to an adult, and to replace cells damaged, depleted or diseased along the way. The DNA molecule separates to form two new molecules. To reproduce, a cell must copy and transmit its genetic information (DNA) to all of its progeny. In doing so, DNA replicates, following a process called semiconservative replication. Each strand of the original molecule acts as a template for the synthesis of a new complementary DNA molecule.

Do you see the pattern and the goal? Do you recognize in yourself the "template" that will be used to replicate yourself in another? Assuming we have matured into the kind of disciples Christ desires, our final task is then to go out and replicate that in others. It's so important that Jesus highlighted it in the last words He said prior to His ascension.

Moving beyond the biology discussion, we saw Jesus do this very thing with people, when He called twelve men to follow Him, eleven of whom would go on to be responsible for thousands of disciples who would then go on to be responsible for making millions of other disciples. This genius replication model has been going on for 2,000 years and is the reason there are nearly two billion Christians alive today and untold millions who have come before us.

Of course, man's ability to carry this process out has been less than perfect which has resulted in an often tepid form of Christian faith and a large segment of the Christian population that goes about their lives making no appreciable contribution to this process of making new disciples. Sometimes, the problem is worse as we often see Christians making the wrong kind of disciples.

My contention in the first lesson in this series, where I described the FLAIR acronym, was that an essential aspect of this five-fold plan was the chronology. We must nail down *following* before we can begin to learn the next thing. And, we must adhere to what we have learned before we can visibly demonstrate to the world Who we are imitating. Only then can we be confidant that we are making disciples the way Jesus desires.

Jesus pointed out this problem in Matthew 23:15.

> *"Woe to you, teachers of the law and Pharisees, you hypocrites! You travel over land and sea to win a single convert, and when you have succeeded, you make them twice as much a child of hell as you are."*

Here He highlights the corrupt nature of making new corrupt disciples when you are not the right type of disciple to begin with. To understand the command for disciples to replicate, we have to go back to the very first book of the bible. The principle for replication is laid down in Genesis 1:28:

> *"God blessed them and said to them, "Be fruitful and increase in*

number; fill the earth and subdue it".

In fact a great portion of the bible's first chapter is involved in replication after our own kind as a product of our fruitfulness (for plants, animals, fish, birds).

Now, fast forward to the Great Commission in Matthew 28:18-20. We are to go and make disciples. Why? Not because we feel like it, but rather because Christ has the authority to dispatch us to do just that (note "*therefore*"). It was important that His authority be injected into the commission here.

Note the key word "*doubted*" in verse 17 of Matthew 28. This is the Greek word *distazo*. It is used here and in Matthew 14:31 (when Peter sank beneath the waves on the Sea of Galilee). Some think this is reference to Thomas' expression of doubt to Jesus post-resurrection, but John tells us that occurred in a house, not on a mountain. In any case, this word for doubt is intentionally different.

In this usage it literally means "to stand in two ways", implying an uncertainty of where or how or why to go. It is not a word that speaks of the absence of faith as much as the abundance of options (placed there by the disciple). Today we might be inhibited from making disciples because we are being distracted by so many other things, and it is only when we are brought to our senses by the authority of Christ in our lives that we can stop vacillating between two or more things. If you will recall from the chapter on "Following", this issue of accepting Christ's authority is one of the key indicators that we are following Him as He intended.

Consider the last message in the Upper Room before Gethsemane. It can be said that the entire teaching of Jesus about His heart for His disciples culminates in the teaching in the Upper Room and can be boiled down to 15 words:

Express our love for Him by obeying Him. Show all men we are His disciples.

I have previously referenced the "three marks of the disciple" that Jesus declared and are recorded in the book of John. This statement above includes the teaching of the first two of those references, which we find in John 8:31 and John 13:35. Now we see Jesus begin His discourse on the last of the three marks of the disciple after John 14:31. Because Jesus beckons them to leave with Him, the setting changes and with it, the emphasis of Jesus' words as well. The final focus is now on fruit-bearing (the third mark) which is not designed to prove our salvation, but rather to demonstrate we are Jesus' disciples and that we understand the purpose He has for us.

Check out a first century map of the city of Jerusalem (there is probably one in the back of your bible). Many scholars believe that the route Jesus and the eleven disciples took to Gethsemane would have taken them past the doors to the Temple. It would have taken them past the Temple and out the Sheep's Gate, down across the Brook Kidron and up to Gethsemane. The Sheep's Gate is just north of the culverts that directed the blood of the lambs being slaughtered for Passover, down to the Brook Kidron.

Consider this: on the night before Jesus, the Lamb of God, would shed His perfect blood for the sins of the world, He would have "passed over" the Brook Kidron which held the ineffectual blood of the lambs that the Jews thought would take care of their sins as they prepared for the Passover the next day. While the world may view that as irony, as Christ-followers we see this as just another exquisite reminder of God's eternal plan, carefully developed long ago and being fully expressed even in something as simple as Jesus' route to the Garden.

Some contend for an alternative route that would take Jesus and His disciples out the southern part of the city. However, John 15 and Jesus' turning of the topic to fruitbearing likely fits better contextually with their path past the door to the Temple. The metal work depicted on the temple door had large gold grape clusters six feet high and a golden vine to represent Israel. The door with its frame was said to be seventy cubits high (that's a little over one hundred feet tall). Jews considered it an honor to be allowed to give gold to be cast as a grape and added to the doors. The vine represented the people of God and the grapes represented the fruit they were to bear.

One problem: they weren't bearing good fruit. Everywhere in the Old Testament where God talks about His "vine" of Israel, it is in a tone that describes the degeneration of the vine and its lack of fruitfulness.

Picture, for a moment, Jesus stopping in front of the great doors and beginning His last teaching (which you can read in John 15:1-8 here in the JB Phillips translation).

> *"I am the real vine, my Father is the vine-dresser. He removes any of my branches which are not bearing fruit and he prunes every branch that does bear fruit to increase its yield. Now, you have already been pruned by my words. You must go on growing in me and I will grow in you. For just as the branch cannot bear any fruit unless it shares the life of the vine, so you can produce nothing unless you go on growing in me. I am the vine itself, you are the branches. It is the man who shares my life and whose life I share who proves fruitful. For the plain fact is that apart from me you can do nothing at all. The man who does not share my life is like a branch that is broken off and withers away. He becomes just like the dry sticks that men pick up and use for the firewood. But if you live your life in me, and my words live in your hearts, you can ask for whatever you like and it will come true for you. This is how my Father will be glorified—in your becoming fruitful and being my disciples.*

Much has been made of this passage as to whom this applies, especially with the imagery of the pruning of some branches and the cutting off of others. There are at least four common views on what this passage is contrasting:

a. Saved versus the lost (Matthew Henry)
b. Israel versus the Church (William Barclay)
c. Saved versus those fallen from grace, for those who hold the errant belief that one can lose their salvation (Drummelow)
d. Fruitful believers versus unfruitful believers (Lawrence Richards).

Considering the context (Jesus with eleven believers who have yet to form the Church), this last option seems most likely, although, many Bible passages such as this can be viewed on multiple levels (e.g., the seven churches of Revelation). Also, Jesus talks about removing branches that are *in Him*. Since branches can't bear fruit apart from Jesus, there is no reason to look at the lost for fruit.

Though this passage has a trove of good theology to investigate, here are the highlights with regard to how God produces fruit in us.

a. **Establishes the relationship**. Matthew, in the Great Commission, focused on the declaration of Jesus "authority". John relates it as establishing a "relationship".

John says Jesus is the True Vine and we are the branches.

b. **Establishes the main theme**: FRUIT. Again in John 15: What is the gardener looking for? Fruit. What do the branches produce? Fruit. What gets you cut off? No fruit. What sets us apart as disciples? Bearing much fruit. Everything is about fruit, even the levels of fruitbearing are significant:

- no fruit (v. 2)
- fruit (v. 2)
- more fruitful (v. 2)
- much fruit (v. 8)

Here we see the progression moving from scarcity toward abundance.

c. **Establishes the way to fruitfulness**: There are two circumstances that provide for our ability to bear fruit. The first is that we must remain in Jesus (abide in Him, or in the parlance of this book, adhere to Him), and the second is being pruned.

Being pruned is a verb that also can mean being "cleansed". The agricultural pruning occurs after a branch has set fruit. All non-fruit bearing branches are then cut off so that the fruit will benefit from more of the sap and nutrients. Pruned branches end up being stronger. This pruning is the way God removes the non-essential and non-productive things in our lives, from a kingdom-works perspective.

How, exactly, does God prune us? There are several methods He employs. The J.B. Phillips translation has it that we are pruned by Jesus' words. Spiritual warfare and suffering persecution can also be methods God allows in order to prune us and make us more fruitful. And often this pruning takes the shape of God actually cutting away other non-essential things in our lives, as a vinedresser cuts away leaves and branches so that the ones that are showing fruitfulness will have the benefit of maximum nutrients flowing through the vine.

The painfulness of this pruning depends on how tightly we are holding on to these things. As a result of pruning, we are released from the type of doubt we spoke of before in Matthew 28:17. As God begins to cut away the things that have made us uncertain of how to proceed as disciple-makers, and as Jesus' words have their own pruning effect, we can no longer "*stand in two ways*". Our course is plotted and we proceed to follow Jesus' command to make new disciples.

Though we can see the advantage of bearing fruit, we might not always see the connection to replicating ourselves because we might not know what shape fruitfulness can take.

Fruit can be conduct (Philippians 1:9-11, fruits of righteousness).
Fruit can be character (Galatians 5:22, fruit of the Spirit).
Fruit can be converts. (John 4:36, fruit for eternal life)

Paul called this last type of fruit "the harvest". More importantly, Jesus gives an indication to this as He continues in John 15:16:

> *"You did not choose me, but I chose you and appointed you to go and bear fruit —fruit that will last. Then the Father will give you whatever you ask in my name."*

The fruit that lasts is eternal fruit and is the saving of souls and the teaching of discipleship (since new disciples will ultimately make more disciples). This fruit of converts depends on the first two types of fruit. You won't have fruit of converts without fruit of conduct and character.

Benefits of Pruning

Since most of us have, at one time or another, pruned a plant, it is not that unusual for us to associate pruning with pain. As I indicated before, it can be painful when we don't surrender ourselves to what God is doing in the pruning. But, with or without pain, our focus must be on the benefits of pruning and the resulting fruit bearing:

- The affirmation from Jesus that we are "clean" (see John 13:10)
- More spiritual nutrients and energy (like the sap in the vine metaphor)

- We get to glorify God (verse 8 of John 15)
- We are visibly and dramatically linked with Christ
- The new privilege of prayer (verses 7 and 16 of John 15).

Add to that the enthusiasm that comes when we successfully make a new convert or effectively assist a new disciple grow into a mature disciple. As with any success, that motivates us to continue in that type of fruit bearing which results in more disciple-makers.

What happens to the branches cut away if they are truly representative of some believers? They are unable to bear fruit, or feel the assurance of abiding in Christ, or enjoy the abundant life that comes from living out God's will, or live a life that clearly points to their discipleship of Christ. Unless...

The Greek for the words "cut off' in John 15 verse 2 is the word *airo.* One of the meanings of this word is "to elevate" or "lift up". This describes the way vine dressers often take unfruitful branches and raise them up or stake them higher to the arbor to promote fruitfulness. Do you know someone who professes to be a believer but is apparently unfruitful in their walk with Jesus? If so, that could be the person God is guiding you toward in order to replicate what He has been doing in you, someone who you could be lifting up toward fruitfulness.

Questions for Discussion

When you think of the term "fruit", what comes to mind in your own life.

Have you considered that part of the fruit Jesus wants you to bear concerns your character?

What part of your character needs special attention so that it can be beneficial toward making "much fruit"?

Chapter Eleven

"When the roots are deep, there is no reason to fear the wind."

–African proverb

A Fragrant Aroma

Recently, I have tried putting more focus on the myriad blessings I am thankful for. I believe that is generally a spiritually healthy thing for all of us to do often as a way of taking an inventory of all that God has done for us. The Apostle Paul writes to Timothy in his first pastoral epistle (chapter 6, verse 17) about our God "who richly provides us with everything for our enjoyment". This type of reflection enables us to express greater appreciation for the "everything".

One blessing that struck me the other day was my five senses. Not only do I experience each of them in a manner that I am thankful for, but we can see that the bible talks a lot about how we are to experience this life using those senses. From "*Taste and see that the Lord is good*" from the Psalms to Jesus inviting Thomas to touch His post-resurrected hands and side, we see examples of how the bible speaks to us in terms that partner with the understanding and appreciation of our senses. One of the most interesting to me is the sense of smell. It is the sense that is dealt with least in the text, but has some of the most interesting references.

As I was pondering this, I started making a list of smells and aromas that were my favorites. The one that came quickest to mind (perhaps because it is an aroma that I smell often) is a particular food: Oscar Meyer DeliFresh Smoked Turkey sandwich meat.

Not Boar's Head, or Buddig, or Hillshire Farms, as good as those brands are. But Oscar Meyer DeliFresh Smoked Turkey. When I am opening up a new package, before I even taste it, I appreciate one of my favorite wonderful aromas.

Or, maybe you are like me and love the smell of fresh, hardwood mulch. Apart from just enjoying the pungent aroma, it instills in me spiritual thoughts, marveling at how God created an ecosystem wherein something that has died and decayed leads to something that is very much alive. Much like the seed that has to die in order to produce many new seeds (John 12:24). I find that a lot of aromas are like this, as they direct our thinking to matters weightier than the simple thing giving off the aroma.

Sometimes those thoughts are cloaked in emotions. The smell of homemade cinnamon rolls on Christmas morning as I lay in bed reminds me, with a glad heart, that my daughter-in-law is up early in the kitchen serving in a way that is soon to make, not just my heart glad, but my stomach glad as well.

Even more often, aromas evoke memories, like how the smell of chlorine reminds me of learning to swim at the YMCA when I was a kid, or the aroma of Aramis cologne reminds me of my father. Smells generally evoke memories more efficiently than all our other senses.

Scientists tell us that is most likely because the area of your brain that analyzes smells (olfactory bulb) is very closely related to the amygdala and hippocampus which are regions of the brain that handle memories. These connections between odors and memories are called the Proust Phenomenon after a novel written by Marcel Proust that featured memories sparked by the smell of a biscuit soaking in tea.

What Others Will Notice In Us

Aromas undoubtedly, then, have a profound effect on people's thinking, emotions, perception and memories. In 2nd Corinthians, we see how Paul describes us in a similar way to impart the importance of our lives relative to those around us. In this passage, we find the only four New Testament references to the word "aroma". The Old Testament has 41 usages, but nearly all of them speak to "an aroma pleasing to the Lord" when describing the various offerings. But, Paul captures the importance of the word "aroma" and uses it to draw a very clear picture of the type of people we, as believers, are to be in this world. Let's take a look at what Paul says in 2nd Corinthians 2.

"[14] But thanks be to God, who always leads us as captives in Christ's triumphal procession and uses us to spread the aroma of the knowledge of him everywhere. [15] For we are to God the pleasing aroma of Christ among those who are being saved and those who are perishing. [16] To the one we are an aroma that brings death; to the other, an aroma that brings life. And who is equal to such a task? [17] Unlike so many, we do not peddle the word of God for profit. On the contrary, in Christ we speak before God with sincerity, as those sent from God."

As a footnote, verse fourteen marks the beginning of what some scholars consider a "digression", which is a common way of writing for Greco-Roman writers of the time. This one extends all the way into chapter seven and contains multiple instances of Paul standing up for his ministry and his authority.

Having used his spiritual authority and his example to teach on forgiveness, Paul now endeavors to teach one other thing about how the believer is to consider his walk and to live out his life, relying again on the authority of his teaching ministry.

First, he draws the reader's attention to the imagery of a triumphant procession.To us this may not have a great impact, but in the Roman world it would. When the Romans had a great victory, they would allow their generals the privilege of a triumphant procession. Here is what it entails:

Conditions:

- General must have been the actual commander in chief

- campaign must have been finished, region pacified and troops brought home (finished!)
- 5,000 of enemy must have fallen in one engagement
- territory must have been extended (not merely attack repelled)
- victory had to be over a foreign foe

Like Jesus with His parables, Paul uses imagery that his audience will be very familiar with and shows how Christ fulfills the role of Commander in Chief who has conquered death.

Historically, the Roman Procession consisted of:

- State officials and senate
- Trumpeters
- Spoils (e.g. when Titus conquered Jerusalem in 70 AD, he brought the candlestick, shewbread table and golden trumpets from the temple)
- Pictures of conquered land and models (ships, citadels)
- white bull for sacrifice
- Captives in chains
- lictors (wardens) with rods
- musicians
- **priests with sweet smelling incense**
- General and his family
- Army yelling "*Triumphe!*"

Catch the significance of the part highlighted in bold. Peter reminds us, in 1 Peter 2, that we are all priests (the priesthood of the believer) and Paul adds to that the idea of carrying an aroma with us. Paul pictures this as Christ's procession against the backdrop of what the world experienced with Rome, and he pictures us as the priests who dispense the aroma that is different for those captives who will be executed versus those who will live in victory. The specific aroma itself is not the point, but the impact of the aroma is.

When we receive Christ as our Savior, we become the recipients of the fragrance of the knowledge of Him. Fragrance is the Greek "*euodia*" which literally means the "sweet smell". Our task, then, is to be the aroma of Christ to the world. "Aroma" is the Greek "*osme*" and literally means "smell". For both those who are saved and those who are not, the same word is used, thus our aroma is the same to each individual. To those who are saved we are a reminder of the life of Victory in Christ.

To those who are not, we are the aroma of death (just as the captives smelled the incense and were no doubt reminded of their impending executions). Being the smell of death may not sound as palatable to us, but it's a cue that unbelievers often require the stark reminder of the spiritual death that awaits them without Christ. It's often the motivator that moves them to consider the Gospel.

Earlier, I regaled you with some of my favorite aromas. Shall I tell you the worst? It occurred at my print shop about 20 years ago when I found a dead and decaying raccoon in the attic of the building. And, when I say "found", I mean I literally popped my head up through the attic door and found its rotting corpse exactly six inches from my face.

"*Disgusting*" is a ridiculously impotent word to describe that moment. Why did I take that action? Because, while going about my work in the shop below, I had begun to smell the aroma of death. And when I did, no other task would supersede getting that aroma out of the area. Of course, it did not help that in removing the carcass, I stepped through the sheetrock of the ceiling and allowed the smell of death to pour even more forcefully into my work area. Try sheetrocking the ceiling with that smell a few inches from your face. It will certainly promote haste in your work.

Some people we encounter will require a more stark reminder of the life and death decision of saying "yes" to Christ's invitation. It's why some people often become more amenable to our message when they face serious health concerns or why people have death bed conversions. The aroma we bring to such encounters is still the aroma of God, but sometimes it evokes in the hearer a final understanding of how death really permeates a faithless life.

Paul closes his passage in 2nd Corinthians 2:16 asking *"And who is equal to such a task?"* People who simply explore this process as a means of profiting by it, as if they were paid motivational speakers (or worse, people who change the truth to suit the paying audience)? NO! Only men and women sent by God (disciples) can bring the sweet aroma of life everlasting to those they encounter. Are you equal to the task? Are you ready to bring the aroma of the knowledge of God to those you meet?

What we should notice in ourselves

While our "aroma" is noticed by others, there is something we should notice about ourselves as we mature in this journey. Just as Jesus often used parts of creation to clarify and amplify his message, a good analogy from the world of botany might help to illuminate what differences we should see in ourselves. Such an example can be seen in Paul's writings to the church at Colossae in Colossians 2:6-7:

> *"[6] Therefore, as you received Christ Jesus the Lord, so walk in him, [7] rooted and built up in him and established in the faith, just as you were taught, abounding in thanksgiving."*

Let's consider what we can learn about the root of a plant in order to flesh out this statement of Paul's. The first root that comes from a plant is called the "radical". For the purposes of our example, it is well named, because it leads us into these radical (as in radically transforming us) stages of our discipleship journey. The root being a part of the plant, and not separate from it, emulates the idea of "abiding" that Jesus emphasized in John 15: 4-5 when he said:

> *"[4]Abide in me, and I in you. As the branch cannot bear fruit by itself, unless it abides in the vine, neither can you, unless you abide in me. [5]I am the vine; you are the branches. Whoever abides in me and I in him, he it is that bears much fruit, for apart from me you can do nothing."*

A root's four major functions are:

- absorption of water and inorganic nutrients. This corresponds to the first two stages of following and learning
- anchoring of the plant body to the ground and supporting it (adhering us securely by virtue of adhering to Christ's teachings)
- storage of food and nutrients (gathering the things we need to steward others as we imitate our Lord)
- vegetative reproduction and competition with other plants (replicating ourselves as disciples).

When these roots are healthy and functioning correctly, the plant grows and is "established" or "built up". As a result, we become steadfast in our walk and well-equipped for the process of making disciples in obedience to our Lord's Great Commission.

Questions for Discussion

What memories resonate with you when you encounter specific aromas?

While disciples don't actually emit a physical aroma different than anyone else, what have you learned about your walk that is most apparent to others?

What part of the metaphor of the root struck you as an area that needs the most attention?

Chapter Twelve

"Joy to the world, the Lord is come.
Let earth receive her King."
–Isaac Watts

Prepare Him Room

In 1719 Isaac Watts penned one of Christendom's most famous songs when he wrote the lyrics to "*Joy to the World*". Drawing inspiration from Psalm 98, and actually pointing more to Jesus' second coming as King (as opposed to His first incarnation as babe in a manger), this song is undoubtedly sung in nearly every church in America, and even around the world during the Christmas holiday season, not to mention in public venues outside the church.

It is in the third line of stanza number one of this popular Christmas carol where we encounter lyrics that are inextricably tied to our life as a disciple of our great King. We have all sung this and other Christmas carols so often, that I fear we do not often just ponder the great words we are singing, and we run past the words so quickly because we are so familiar with "*Joy to the World*".

Let every heart "prepare Him room"...

Have we thought about what that means and what commitment we are verbalizing when we sing it? It is so ingrained in our deep search to grow as disciples that we sometimes need to be brought back to the very simple notion that being a disciple of Jesus begins with preparing room for Him in our hearts.

This, of course, demands that we not only make a choice about what fills our heart but also make choices about what things will no longer command valuable spiritual square footage that belongs to our King. Both are part of the preparing. And both are part of the continuing process of readying necessary space for what we learn and experience as we grow along the continuum that we call discipleship and as we are sanctified, or set apart, for God's good purposes.

The word "room" has some very interesting and important usages in the New Testament. Perhaps the most significant, with respect to the above instruction, is seen in Luke 22:

> *"[7] Then came the day of Unleavened Bread on which the Passover lamb had to be sacrificed. [8] Jesus sent Peter and John, saying, "Go and make preparations for us to eat the Passover." [9] "Where do you want us to prepare for it?" they asked. [10] He replied, "As you enter the city, a man carrying a jar of water will meet you. Follow him to the house that he enters, [11] and say to the owner of the house, 'The Teacher asks: Where is the guest room, where I may eat the Passover with my disciples?' [12] He will show you a large room upstairs, all furnished. Make preparations there."*

In His disciples, Jesus is looking for "large" rooms (spacious by virtue of clearing out things from the space that will encumber our growth as followers of Jesus), "furnished" (the Greek here indicates a couch or straw furnishing for a bed, clearly a place of relaxation and peace) that is an "upper" room (above and separated from the ground or the world and one that is the pinnacle of our hierarchy). But most importantly, we see that it is a place that Jesus already knows about, indeed He has already planned for. Your heart was designed as a place for preparations to be made for the King.

Questions for Discussion

Has the analogy of your heart to a room that Jesus wants to occupy given you any ideas of how you can make that space more available and useful to our Lord?

How does the idea of your heart being a "furnished room" for Jesus impact your thinking about your life as a disciple?

Is Christ maintaining the highest spot (the upper part) of the hierarchy of your heart?

Chapter Thirteen

"There is the moment of surrender,
and there is a practice of surrender."
–Patrick Morley

Taking on Water

While I expect that the vast majority of folks who read this book are people who have already started their walk of faith with Christ, it would be short-sighted of me not to acknowledge that there may be some of you who have picked this book up out of curiosity. Or, on a recommendation from a friend. Thankfully, you have made your way this far, even though you started without the benefit of of having trusted Christ with your life...yet. If that describes you, let me humbly thank you for your courage to plunge into something like this that is undoubtedly foreign to your life, and for staying with it to the end. My hope and prayer is that this has stirred up many questions in you and that, as a result, you are opening yourself up to God Who wants to reveal Himself to you, and to the opportunity for the greatest decision you will ever make in this lifetime.

Hopefully, this book has described a lifestyle that, though challenging, is also alluring in the best way because it is optimally meaningful. Perhaps you are beginning to recognize that this message fills a hole in you that you have been aware of all your life, despite your inability on your own to fill it in any way that even approaches satisfaction. Let me make a way to continue our conversation by sharing with you my email at the end of this chapter where you can write me and continue the conversation that has begun in this book; asking questions, sharing your experience reading this book and perhaps securing more help in finding the narrow path that emerges from the narrow gate.

In the same vein, you may be someone with some insecurities about your faith or a past profession of that faith, and after reading these pages you realize your walk looks nothing like it ought to or, more importantly, how it can look. Perhaps your life would be better described as one that is "taking on water" instead of one that is "taking on provisions" for the life God has planned for you. For you, I would echo the words of the Apostle Paul from 2 Corinthians 13:5:

> *"Examine yourselves to see whether you are in the faith; test yourselves. Do you not realize that Christ Jesus is in you—unless, of course, you fail the test?"*

Here, Paul is writing to believers, so he is not questioning their conversion as much as he is calling them to a self-inquiry to see if their profession matches what should be expected of a Christ follower.

In this passage, the word "examine" is the Greek word *peirazo*, which is usually translated as "tempt" or "try" or "test". Here, it has the meaning of "**assaying**" which is defined as the testing of metals.

Assaying usually occurs not to prove something is metal, but rather to prove how valuable the metal is and what the characteristics are that make it worthy. In the same way, when we examine ourselves, we are setting out not to prove we are saved (although this may be one of the initial critical examinations for someone whose life does not yet match their profession), but rather to prove where we are on the journey, which Paul is praying for his people. In other words, it results in the question "*do I look like a genuine Christian?*" Emphasis here is on the word "genuine".

It is possible that you may be one of those people that somewhere in the past you spoke words that indicated a change, but by laying your life up against the demands of the narrow path as expressed in the previous pages, you realize that your life does not represent that well. You have not been experiencing the transformative power of the gospel that is not only big enough to save you, but is also a gospel big enough to live in. If that's the case, here's good news for you!

Right now, your heavenly Father awaits you to secure your place in His kingdom by genuinely giving your heart to Him. In that moment He will justify you and save you and then set your feet on the narrow path for a lifetime of preparing you and gifting you and setting you apart in this world for the plans He has for you. If that is happening to you now, I invite you to drop me an email and let me know, share your experience, or seek prayer.

Finally, if you are certain you have done that business with God in the past, I hope most of you who read this book will do two things: 1) identify where on the continuum of spiritual growth you are on your journey of the narrow path, and begin to put into practice an orderly approach of living and growing "aright". And 2) I hope you will share this book with someone who you desire to disciple or who you feel can benefit from this roadmap to spiritual maturity.

Over the last thirty-five years I have had the distinct privilege to teach the Word of God on a small platform in the local church. I estimate I have shared this teaching with over 1,000 people over the years and you cannot imagine how fulfilling that has been. Now, at this stage in my life, I sense in my spirit that God is leading me to extend this teaching to a much larger platform.

As a printing business owner for more than forty years, I have developed an adept understanding of the process for printing books that you can hold in your hand and place on your library shelves. Now, with the advent of e-publishing and printing-on-demand these last few years, the challenges of printing and marketing physical books has been overcome with the ease of publishing digital books that can be effortlessly distributed around the globe, or printing books one at a time as they are purchased.

This is where you come in one final time. Your willingness to share and recommend this book to others aids in my ability to obediently extend my understanding of God's Word to a much bigger platform. In addition, your assistance holds the potential to see lives changed as believers are properly set upon the path to mature discipleship.

Each year, I read about 100 novels in my spare time. And, at the end of each is a sort of apologetic epilogue, requesting the reader go online to the bookseller and leave a review. These reviews dramatically elevate a book's visibility to future readers. And so, I am going to make one last request, unapologetically: please leave an authentic review. By that I mean, if it is a great book or, in your opinion, even if it's an average book, please say that in your review so that others can be well-informed when they give in to their curiosity about *The Narrow Path*.

Thank you in advance!

Contact me at tommy@layman2layman.com.

Questions for Discussion

Thinking back over the entire book, what most resonated with you about the narrow path you are on?

What new truth was illuminated in a way that it will make a dramatic impact on your walk with Jesus?

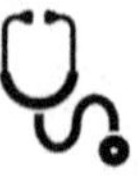

What needs to be your next step in preparing yourself for this great journey?

www.ingramcontent.com/pod-product-compliance
Lightning Source LLC
LaVergne TN
LVHW050641100826
845148LV00011B/1931

* 9 7 8 1 6 8 4 8 8 1 7 7 2 *